HOW TO
Study
THE *Bible*
Yourself FOR

TIM LaHAYE

HARVEST HOUSE
PUBLISHERS
EUGENE, OREGON 97402

Published in association with the literary agency of *Alive Communications, Inc.,* 1465 Kelly Johnson Blvd., Suite #320, Colorado Springs, CO 80920.

Cover by Koechel Petersen & Associates, Minneapolis, Minnesota

HOW TO STUDY THE BIBLE FOR YOURSELF

ISBN 1-56865-813-3

Printed in the United States of America.

Dedication

This new updated edition is dedicated to Mike Fuller, Billy Shields, and Ken ("Hutch") Hutcheson, the three San Diego Charger football players who had the most to do with starting a Bible study that lasted at least three years. During that time several players made professions of faith in Christ, several found new purpose for their lives, one estranged couple was reunited, and almost all the participants were helped as they went through some of the trials and disappointments of professional sports, from serious injuries to being cut or traded. All who studied faithfully were helped to prepare for life after football.

It's hard to believe that was 20 Super Bowls ago. Mike and Billy are Christian businessmen and fathers now; Ken is a very successful pastor in Seattle. These young men found that whether in football or life, we all need to study the Bible for ourselves. Mike and his wife, Penny, came to us as newlyweds, and now they have three children. All of us were prayerfully concerned as we watched Mike, the fastest defensive back and punt-return specialist on the team for ten years, become reduced by cancer to a shadow of his former self. But Mike and Penny faithfully trusted in God during this experience, and we rejoiced as we saw him miraculously recover and continue to serve his Lord. The principles given in this book will help anyone to prepare for whatever future circumstances life has in store for him or her.

Contents

1

You Can
Understand the Bible!

A 17-year-old young man went to church for the first time because the shoe salesman who had led him to Christ told him he needed to learn more about the Savior he had just received. After the song service the minister said, "Turn to First Timothy 5:12."

The young convert turned to the first page of the Bible which his friend had given him and thumbed through Genesis, Exodus, Deuteronomy, Joshua, and a number of other books but could not find Timothy. Turning to the table of contents he found that First Timothy was on page 325, but when he found that page number he was in the book of Joshua. Again looking into the table of contents he discovered that there were *two* basic sections of the Bible, and that First Timothy was in the second section! By the time the young Christian had found the text the minister was finished with his sermon. Needless to say, the young man was embarrassed and a little befuddled.

Have you ever felt like that? If so, don't be discouraged, because most new Christians start out the same way. From that discouraging beginning the young man developed a desire to know the Bible thoroughly. Years later he became a famous preacher who, it is said, led one million people to Jesus Christ. In the later years of his life he founded a Bible institute that today trains over 1200 young people annually in the Word of God. This young man's name was Dwight L. Moody, and few men have ever influenced Christianity more than he did. But he would never have been an influence at all had he not been willing to study the Word of God for himself!

Although we don't know what method Moody used to study the Bible, we do know that he was not given much formal education, and that most of his Bible study he did on his own. The methods outlined in this book are probably similar to the ones he used. You too can be an effective servant of Christ—but only if you are willing to study the Bible for yourself.

Success or failure in the Christian life depends on how much of the Bible you get into your mind on a regular basis and how obedient you are to it. True, you can go to heaven knowing little more than John 3:16 and Romans 10:9,10, because God's marvelous gift of salvation is so free that all you have to do to get it is to receive it by faith (John 1:12). But if you are ever going to be a happy, successful Christian it will be by regularly feeding on the Word of God, and that takes work. The more you work at it the faster and better you will grow, and this growth is well worth the price it requires.

Jesus Christ gave the formula for success when He said, "If ye know these things, happy are ye if ye do them" (John 13:17). *Happiness is the result of knowing and doing the will of God as He has revealed it in the Bible.* The problem with so many Christians today is that they don't spend much time learning the principles of the Bible, so they don't even know what is expected of them. No wonder they don't enjoy all the blessings of the Christian life!

The Bible Was Written for People

Unfortunately, many Christians have the idea that they cannot understand the Bible. They think it was written for theologians or ministers, so all they do is listen to "Bible scholars" lecture and preach or read books about the Bible, but they spend very little time actually studying it for themselves. The sad thing about this is that the Bible wasn't written for theologians but for people just like you! For example, the Lord said through the apostle John, "I write unto you, *little children*, because your sins are forgiven you...[and] because ye have known the Father" (1 John 2:12,13). Even "little children" or brand-new Christians can understand the Bible. This means that *you* can understand the Bible! You may not be able to go down into the depths of Bible truth the way the scholars do, and there will be a few things you won't fully understand, but you will find far more in Scripture that you *can* understand than what you cannot.

Once the fact that you can study the Bible for yourself really grips you, your Christian life will take on an entirely new dimension. I have watched new Christians and some old believers who had never been very excited about their Christian experience really come to life by studying the Bible on their own. Through the years I have developed a very simple method of Bible study that has literally transformed the lives of those who have used it consistently. This book was written to help you study the Word of God and to experience that same kind of transforming Christian experience.

But there is one thing I must tell you: Study is work. A Greek mathematician once said, "There is no royal road to geometry." This statement was made to a young student who wondered if there was an easier way of learning than to study. But of course there isn't, and the same is true for Bible study. In fact, it takes the hardest kind of work there is: *thinking*. But if you follow the program outlined in this book, you will find the effort well worth it, for you will develop a working knowledge of the Bible that will not only enrich your own spiritual life but will enable you to serve Jesus Christ effectively for years to come.

The idea for this method of study really came to me some years ago when I read an advertisement in a magazine that said, "Learn English in 15 minutes a day." Nothing had been harder for me in high school than English! But this man showed me it could be mastered in just 15 minutes a day. Actually, you can master almost anything in 15 minutes a day if you do it long enough. This program will take 15 minutes a day for reading, another 15 minutes a day for studying, and some spare moments for learning. By the end of three years you will have accomplished the following:

1. Read the Bible completely through.
2. Read the key books several times.
3. Accumulated the major principles, promises, and commands of Scripture.
4. Studied the most important chapters.
5. Learned a number of key verses.
6. Developed a working knowledge of the Bible.
7. Developed a lifetime habit of Bible study that will enrich your entire life.

I assume that you regularly attend a Bible-teaching church where you hear the Bible taught, and of course you should continue in this. But now I suggest that you add the other four methods of Bible study: *reading, studying, learning,* and *thinking.* You will find the results well worth the time invested!

What Bible Study Will Do for You

Before we get into the mechanics of Bible study we should take a moment to see if it is really worth all the time you are going to invest in it. You have a legitimate right to ask, "What will 15 minutes a day spent reading the Bible and 15 minutes a day studying it do for me?" Consider the following.

**1.
It will make
you a strong
Christian**

No one wants to be a weakling, whether physically or spiritually. The "young men" of 1 John 2:14 were no longer "children" but were "strong" because the Word of God lived in them and they overcame the wicked one. This means they had fed on the Word of God until they had grown strong enough in the faith that they were not continually defeated by sin and temptation. There is only one possible way to grow strong spiritually—by reading and studying the Word of God.

Through the years I have watched thousands of Christians—some brilliant, some average, some with college backgrounds; some were scarcely educated, and some had gone to Bible college, but most had not. From each of these groups I have seen some Christians remain continual babies while others have grown strong in the Lord. The thing they had in common was not their mutual gifts of education but *whether or not they developed the habit of daily feeding their mind on the Word of God.* Note the expression in 1 John 2:14 "ye have overcome the wicked one." This takes spiritual strength that comes only from a study of the Word of God. Of the hundreds of spiritual failures I have counseled, the thing they all had in common was an absence of the Word in their daily lives. All these failures (and consequent miseries) could have been avoided if these people had learned to study the Word for themselves.

2.
It will assure
you of
salvation

The first thing every young Christian needs is to be absolutely certain he is a Christian. Salvation is so marvelous—a free gift from a loving God—that it seems too good to be true. Consequently one of the first difficulties a new convert runs into after he has left the one who led him to Christ is entertaining doubts about his salvation. The *only source* of assurance is the Bible! But what good is this to him if he doesn't read the Bible for himself? The promises and guarantees of God are of little value hidden between the covers of a Bible; Christians need them on the frontal lobes of their brain. And that is the reason the Bible was written. Listen to 1 John again, chapter 5, verse 13: "These things have I written unto you that believe on the name of the Son of God, *that ye may know that ye have eternal life*" (emphasis added).

The Christian who has an abiding assurance that he is a child of God and that God is *his* heavenly Father has the basis for a sound emotional life. The vast majority of Christians with fears, worries, and other emotional foibles lack assurance of salvation because they have been heeding their minds instead of reading their Bibles. No one will be assured of God when he is limited to the thoughts of his mind, because as the Bible teaches, the concept of God does not come by thinking, but by the "wisdom of God" in Scripture (1 Corinthians 1:21). If you want to enjoy the assurance of your salvation, then begin to study the Word of God regularly, for this is the only place you will find it.

**3.
It will give
you
confidence
and power in
prayer**

Now that you are a Christian you can talk to your heavenly Father about anything you have on your heart. But how do you know He is listening? Because He says so in His Word—in many places. First John 5:14,15 teaches that we can pray in confidence that He hears us. In John 15:7 our Lord promised, "If ye abide in me, and my words abide in you, ye shall ask what ye will, and it shall be done unto you." This means that Bible study (which is how His words abide in us) gives us power in prayer, because as we study God's Word we become acquainted with His will and consequently learn how to pray.

Confucius was once asked by one of his students, "Does it help to pray for our sins?" to which he is said to have replied, "I'm not sure, but it can't hurt to try." That is no help at all! Only the Bible teaches that God does in fact answer prayer, and only the Bible-taught Christian fully enjoys that confidence.

**4.
It will cleanse
you from sin**

Lady Macbeth was not the first to cry out in anguish of soul because of the guilt-consciousness of her sin. Guilt is a universal problem, and billions of people have no idea where to go for cleansing. But guilt should never bother a Bible-taught Christian because our Lord said, "Now ye are clean through the word which I have spoken unto you" (John

15:3). The Word of God has a cleansing effect upon the believer. Our Lord prayed, "Sanctify them through thy truth; thy word is truth" (John 17:17). The Word of God has a powerful cleansing effect on the Christian who studies it.

A father was once asked by his son to explain how the Word of God cleansed a person. Instead of answering, he asked his son to take a wicker basket down to the lake and bring him a basketful of water. The lad tried several times, but before he got back to where his dad was, the basket was empty. In frustration he complained to his father, "It's impossible—before I get it here the water has all run out!" The father then called the boy's attention to how clean the basket was and said, "That is how the Word of God cleanses the believer as it passes through his mind."

How do we know that our sins are forgiven? Because the Bible says, "If we confess our sins, he is faithful and just to forgive us our sins, and to cleanse us from all unrighteousness" (1 John 1:9). What encouragement it gives us to know that God is faithful in the work of cleansing!

As a young Christian, you need to know what is sin and what is not. God has not left you to your own judgment. He says, "Wherewithal shall a young man cleanse his way? By taking heed thereto according to the word" (Psalm 119:9). Studying the Bible will cleanse you from sin and warn you of sin.

When I was a young Christian, I asked a visiting minister to sign my Bible, which he did, but he also added a note that is very perceptive: "This book will keep you from sin or sin will keep you from this book."

5.
It will give
you joy

One of the blessings of the Christian life is joy, but often that joy is stifled by the problems of life. Our Lord said, "These things have I spoken unto you that my joy might remain in you, and that your joy might be full" (John 15:11). If you read the writings of mankind or look at the problems that surround you, your joy will turn to fear, dread, or sometimes depression.

During a financial recessionary period I attended a meeting of the church board of trustees. As I listened to the men talk it sounded like the Lord had gone out of business—all they did was forecast gloom, doom, and despair. Finally I asked, "What have you men been reading lately?" They replied, "*The Wall Street Journal, U.S. News and World Report, The San Diego Union*," etc. So I replied, "You've been reading the wrong material!" It is the *Word of*

God that puts joy in our heart regardless of the circumstances.

6.
It will
produce peace
in
your life

One of the supernatural evidences of the Christian life is peace in one's heart when the circumstances of life call for worry and anxiety. Now that you have received Christ as your Savior and Lord you have a right to expect to be different, and your friends are justified in expecting to see that difference. When a supernatural power like the Holy Spirit comes to live in your life, you will be different. That difference is primarily shown in your emotions, which will be characterized by peace in the face of difficulties. But if the Word of God does not "dwell in you richly" by reading and study, it will not produce the peace that should characterize your life.

Jesus Christ said, "These things have I spoken unto you that in me ye might have peace. In the world ye shall have tribulation; but be of good cheer, I have overcome the world" (John 16:33). What makes this statement of particular interest is that our Lord gave this message to His disciples just before the turmoil that resulted in His crucifixion. As His disciples faced this impending crisis, He wanted them to have *peace* through His Word.

For almost 2000 years now God's people have fortified themselves for the crises of life by reading and studying the Bible. That's what God meant when He said, "Let the peace of God rule in your hearts, to which also ye are called in one body, and be ye thankful" (Colossians 3:15). Peace is not automatic. We let it flood our hearts through filling our minds with the promises, principles, and faithfulness of God as taught in His Word. Many a Christian businessman who reads the *Wall Street Journal* or *Time* magazine daily instead of his Bible becomes upset at monetary conditions, when all the time God wants to flood his heart with peace through the daily reading of His Word.

7. It will guide you in making important decisions of life.

Life is filled with decisions—little ones, big ones, and many in between. When the principles of God are well-known to a Christian, this simplifies the process of decision-making. That's what Scripture means when it says, "Thy word is a lamp unto my feet and a light unto my path" (Psalm 119:105). The principles of God serve as a guide in reaching decisions.

Today's "situation ethics" philosophy is a chaotic approach to life that produces much harm. It is far better to program biblical principles into your mind in advance of a crisis than to wait until emotions, passions, and life pressures close in on you and then try to decide what to do. As the Lord Himself said,

"Blessed [happy] are they that hear the word of God and keep it" (Luke 11:28). You cannot keep what you have not heard! But as you fill your mind daily with the Word of God it will enlighten the dark paths of the future with divine guidance.

8.
It will enable you to articulate your faith

Most of the people you meet in life are ignorant of Bible concepts. Many of these have questions or doubts and need someone who knows the Bible to guide them. God challenges us, "Sanctify the Lord God in your hearts, and be ready always to give an answer to every man that asketh you a reason of the hope that is in you, with meekness and fear" (1 Peter 3:15). The only way you will be able to answer the questioner, scorner, or sincere seeker of truth is to be "ready always to answer" them by daily reading and studying the Word. A Navy lieutenant I counseled who claimed to have been a Christian 11 years said, "I never have an opportunity to share my faith with anyone." It seemed incredible to me that a man stationed aboard an aircraft carrier with 3000 other men couldn't find someone to share Christ with, but I ignored his comment and started him on a Bible reading, studying, and learning program.

Two months later when he came in for his weekly checkup he told me about leading his first soul to Christ. Then he reminded me of his previous comment and said, "My problem wasn't lack of opportunity; I just didn't know what to do when one came along. Now my mind is so filled with the Word of God that I'm sharing it all the time. Before I started studying the Bible I just didn't know what to say." That young man's experience could be multiplied many times, for you cannot communicate what you do not know. Almost every Christian wants to be fruitful and to effectively share Christ with others, but this is totally impossible without at least an elementary knowledge of the Word of God.

9. It will guarantee your success!

Everyone wants to be successful. This doesn't mean we all want riches or fame; you can have those without having true success. We all yearn to succeed in our chosen field of endeavor; that's why "how-to" or "success-oriented" books are so popular today. No one reads books on how to fail! Joshua 1:8 tells us, "This book of the law shall not depart out of thy mouth, but thou shalt meditate therein day and night, that thou mayest observe to do according to all that is written therein; for then thou shalt make thy way prosperous, and then thou shalt have good success." Note the words "and then thou shalt have good success." Daily meditation (thinking) on the Word of God produces the success that everyone desires. Certainly it did for Joshua.

Many Christian businessmen have claimed this same promise and today testify to God's faithfulness.

Lest you think that God's promise to Joshua was an isolated one, we should look at the formula for happiness found in the first psalm: "Blessed is the man that walketh not in the counsel of the ungodly, nor standeth in the way of sinners, nor sitteth in the seat of the scornful. But his delight is in the law of the Lord, and in his law doth he meditate day and night. And he shall be like a tree planted by the rivers of water, that bringeth forth its fruit in its season; his leaf also shall not wither, and whatsoever he doeth shall prosper" (Psalm 1:1-3). That kind of daily productivity comes from daily feeding one's mind on the Word of God.

Unfortunately, many Christians think they are too busy to refresh their minds each day on the Word of God. What they don't realize is that a daily quiet time costs them nothing in the long run because the rest of their day will be more successful than if they had ignored their Bible. A brilliant neurosurgeon in Atlanta claims, "The most important part of my day is the first 30 minutes after awaking, so I spend 20 minutes of it reading and studying the Word of God. It enriches the rest of my day." Try it—you'll like it!

3

How to
Read the Bible

For all practical purposes, reading is the foundation of all learning. Someone has said, "If you can read you can learn anything." If you are going to learn the Bible, you will have to develop the habit of reading large portions of the Scriptures. Bible study is essential to become "approved unto God" (2 Timothy 2:15). But the foundation of that study must be reading. We will distinguish between devotional reading and study reading. The latter will be discussed at length later in this book.

It has been my observation that unless a person has the regular habit of reading the Bible, he will never develop a regular study habit. In fact, it is usually the consistent practice of reading the Scriptures that inspires a person to become a student of the Book. I have never met a person who enjoyed studying the Bible who had not first developed the habit of regularly reading it.

One of the advantages of reading the Bible is that you don't get so bogged down in the complexities of verse or word analysis that you lose the overall purpose and meaning of the writer. These detailed methods of study, which we will cover later, should not be attempted until you are acquainted with the main theme—and that is only possible by reading the whole book. G. Campbell Morgan, a popular Bible commentator of another generation, used to say he would not attempt to teach any book of the Bible until he had read it 50 times. He felt it took that many readings to properly relate all of the parts to the whole.

To gain the most value from your reading, consider carefully the following techniques.

1.
Read daily

Daily Bible reading is to your spiritual life what daily eating is to your physical life. We are all familiar with the necessity of regular mealtimes. If we skip meals or rush them, their primary values are lost. Just as the body needs a regular feeding time to maintain its energy level, so the spiritual man must regularly be fed the Word of God. Job compared the two in 23:12: "Neither have I gone back from the commandment of his lips; I have esteemed the words of his mouth more than my necessary food."

Most people find that the morning is the best time to read the Word devotionally. It is easier to program Bible reading into your schedule in the morning because all you have to do is get up 15 minutes earlier to get your 15-minute reading done. If you are a morning person, one who wakes up bright and alert, it is particularly advisable to do it then, for it gets your day off to a good start. If, however, you are a night person like some of the rest of us, your brain isn't too alert early in the morning. If you function best at night, it might be advisable to do your reading after dinner or before retiring.

The biggest problem with setting your daily Bible reading (or quiet time) at night is that if you forget it or a change of schedule necessitates that you miss the regular time, it is difficult to work it in later. The most common time, early in the morning, provides ample substitute scheduling, if the regular time must be skipped.

Whatever the time, it has been my observation that if you don't set one, your good intentions will never be realized and you will only occasionally read your Bible.

2.
Set a regular reading time

"How much time should I devote to reading the Bible each day?" It's a question I hear frequently. My answer depends on my appraisal of the seriousness and discipline of the individual. If I suspect he is a good starter and poor finisher, I say "at least five minutes." I would rather have him consistent at five minutes a day than consistent at nothing. But frankly, if you mean business with God and really want to develop a working knowledge of the Word, you had better plan on a minimum of 15 minutes daily.

When you think about it, that isn't too much. Most people spend that long reading the newspaper or watching newscasts on TV, or spend that long unnecessarily on the telephone. In addition, we usually spend more time than that three times a day feeding our bodies.

Our three-year program of providing you with a working knowledge of the Bible is based on at least 15 minutes of reading and 15 minutes of studying each day over a three-year period. I don't see how the average person will ever develop an adequate knowledge of the Word on less than that.

Most of those who have followed this procedure indicated that after the first or second month they developed the reading habit to the extent that frequently they became so engrossed with God's message to them that they lost track of time and read much longer than the minimum 15 minutes.

3.
Set a
regular place

It will help your concentration and consistency if you set a regular place to do your 15 minutes or more of daily reading. All speed-reading experts recommend that reading be done in a sitting position and preferably at a desk, as it aids in concentration. Another thing it does is eliminate other visual distractions. The less you have on your desk besides your Bible while reading, the better. Coming regularly to this "quiet place" helps establish the devotional mood.

4.
Read with
a pencil at hand

The biggest danger to devotional Bible reading is in letting your eyes run across the words and assuming you have read the material. Many Christians spend the allotted 15 minutes each day, follow their reading with prayer, and assume they have had an effective quiet time. But if you asked them one hour later what they had read, they wouldn't have the foggiest idea. Their eyes read the words but their brain wasn't turned on.

The best way to dial your brain into a vital attitude is to pick up a pencil and be ready to receive a message from God. That very act makes you more alert and expectant that God will communicate something to you today which you need to know. Another thing it does is assist your memory. An educator once said, "There is no learning without written duplication." When you see something special in your reading, write it down. Not only does this record it for handy review in the future, but it also helps to cement the thought more forcibly into your brain.

5. Read devotionally

The Bible is a living Book written by a loving God to His children and it is "profitable" (practical). In it He provides basic principles, guidance, and inspiration on how to live. It was written to people, and because human nature hasn't changed in the years since its writing, it has a message for God's people today. More than a message, however, the Bible is true soul food.

Man is not just body, mind, and emotions, as most humanists indicate, but he has a strong spiritual side to his nature also! That area of his being is indwelt at salvation as a "new creature": "Therefore, if any man be in Christ, he is a new creation; old things are passed away; behold, all things are become new" (2 Corinthians 5:17). This area must be fed from that time on. Consequently, even when a person doesn't find anything special in his reading (and some days will be like that) there is still an aspect of spiritual benefit just in the reading, for it feeds this devotional or spiritual side of our being.

The best way to read the Word of God devotionally is to prayerfully ask God for some message for today. Many times He will give you a thought that answers the hunger of your heart. Sometimes He will give you a blessing that you will need later in the day. In either case it will be helpful to write it down, as suggested above. Take special care, however, to see that the thought is true. We will go into this in detail later, but a verse should never be lifted out of its setting to provide a special message today when by doing so it contradicts the sense of the whole passage.

Remember, the Bible was written in paragraphs, not verses. The verse divisions were added about 1500 years after the Scripture was completed, and although they are handy aids to finding special messages and teachings, it is dangerous for them to be lifted out of context. The Holy Spirit is the Author of the Bible, and He is the One who inspires us with a devotional message from God as we read it. He will *never* lead us to use a portion of His Word that is contrary to His will or in conflict with His original meaning.

Devotional reading provides the spiritual inspiration for daily living that every Christian needs, and it is always based on the truth revealed in the Bible.

6.
Keep a daily
spiritual diary

The best single tool I have used (or helped others to use) to get the greatest blessing out of devotional reading is to establish the habit of keeping a daily spiritual diary. When the idea of keeping a diary first came to me I rejected it because I'm not the diary-keeping type. But as I wrote down my thoughts from God found in my daily Bible reading, diary-keeping seemed to naturally fall into place. Since then I have shared this practice with hundreds of Christians who really want to deepen their spiritual lives and enrich their relationship to God. Many have testified that it has proven the most inspirational tool they have ever used.

A fancy diary or notebook is not necessary; an ordinary sheet of paper or a small spiral notebook will suffice. Allowing one page per day, put the day of the week, the month, and the date on top, with space for the text to be read. In a Bible class I taught for 47 students who were required to keep a daily diary, I discovered 47 different formats when I collected them at the end of the term! Some were ornate and elaborate, others were simplicity itself. The important thing was that they were done! In this book there is a sample of a Spiritual Diary first produced by Family Life Seminars. You would be wise to begin by using this format and then later develop your own system.

What to Include in Your Spiritual Diary

As shown in the accompanying sample diary, there are five things you should include in your diary.

1. God's message to you today

The first thing to look for is that special message from God for the day. Naturally, this will be influenced largely by the passage under study for that day and your own particular need at the time.

2. A promise from God

The Bible is filled with promises from God to His children. You won't find one in every passage, but they are so common that you will locate one very frequently. In many passages you will find several, and for that reason you should select the best one from the three or four chapters you read that day. There are two things to consider in claiming promises: 1) Make sure they are universal promises, and 2) make sure they apply to you. Some are for Israel, some are for the people in the millennium, and some are promised judgments on the wicked. The little chorus that used to be popular in Sunday school, "Every promise in the book is mine," just isn't true. As a rule, the context will indicate clearly whether it is for you or someone else.

Another thing to keep in mind when looking for promises is whether there are any conditions to the promise. For example, a recent heresy has become quite popular in some circles based on the promise that God "is faithful and just to forgive us our sins and to cleanse us from all unrighteousness," according to 1 John 1:9. They suggest that anytime a Christian sins he is automatically forgiven. It is difficult for most of us to understand why those who hold this idea do not read the condition clearly stated in that verse: "*If* we confess our sins he is faithful and just to forgive us our sins and to cleanse us from all unrighteousness." We must confess our sins (admit to God they were wrong) or they will not be forgiven. Never claim a promise from God unless you are willing to meet the conditions listed. You should always write down the conditions that precede a promise so you will know whether or not it is legitimate for you to claim.

3.
A command
to keep

The Bible is filled with commands for God's people to obey. These commands are for our good, since the keeping of them both lengthens and enriches our lives. As you come upon these commands in your reading, you will be forced to select the most important of them for your life at that moment and enter it into your diary.

4.
A timeless
principle

One of the reasons the Bible is the greatest manual on human behavior ever written is because it contains thousands of timeless principles for daily living. These are divine insights that guide the believer and help program his mind in advance so that when decisions are to be made he doesn't have to go through an agonizing thought process to make a decision. Consider some samples:

> Whatsoever a man soweth, that shall he also reap (Galatians 6:7).

> Humble yourselves therefore under the mighty hand of God, that he may exalt you in due time (1 Peter 5:6).

> Be ye not unequally yoked together with unbelievers (2 Corinthians 6:14).

Obeying these and many other timeless principles is what produces happiness and fulfillment in the lives of God's people. The last command listed above saved a printer I know over $40,000 of debts when offered a "good deal" by another printer who was not a Christian. One week after refusing to get involved with this unbeliever in a partnership, the fraud he was almost a part of was revealed.

Many Christians have saved themselves from an unfortunate marriage by applying the timeless principle in that verse. There are principles in the Bible on almost every subject in the world, and by listing one in your daily diary each day you will have over 300 by the end of your first year.

**5.
Your
application**

As a principal tool in implementing the above "finds" in your daily reading, pick out one that is in the area of your greatest need and list how you intend to implement it in your daily life. For example, suppose your command for the day is "Husbands, love your wives, even as Christ also loved the church . . ." (Ephesians 5:25). Pick some area where you know you have been selfish with your partner and write in a sentence how you plan to be more loving. By asking God's help you will find that not only will your spiritual life improve but your relationship with your wife will be enhanced.

This kind of simple but practical application to your life of the daily challenges you find in God's Word will definitely transform your life into the kind of growing, consistent Christian walk that every child of God needs. We will say more later about applying God's truth to your life.

Reasons for Keeping a Spiritual Diary

There are many reasons for keeping a daily spiritual diary, but consider especially the following five reasons.

1.
It provides a handy method for recording special daily insight from God's Word

Good intentions are fine, but unless you have an organized plan for implementing them you will never prove consistent in your devotional life, and without one there is little chance for spiritual maturity and success in your life. But a handy spiritual diary kept near your Bible makes it easy for you to get off by yourself with a pencil and spend at least 15 profitable minutes with God each day.

2.
It produces an attitude of expectancy

Unless you plan to enter something into a notebook or diary, your daily quiet time often becomes drudgery. Keeping a daily spiritual diary develops a mental attitude of expectancy that not only attunes your brain for diligent thought but helps with consistency by producing a spirit of anticipation that today you will hear from God.

3.
It provides a handy check on regularity

In a glance you can tell just how consistent you are in your quiet time, for the skipping of days is readily apparent. Many Christians think they are more consistent in their devotions than they really are; the daily spiritual diary will keep you honest.

**4.
It provides a
handy review**

One of the blessings in keeping a daily diary is that in a few minutes each week you can review the "cream" of your devotional reading for the week and month. This review further helps to cement the Word of God in your mind.

**5.
It provides
an easy
appraisal of
spiritual
growth**

By the time you have kept a spiritual diary for three months, you will be amazed at how much more mature you have become. At first you skim the surface with your findings, but gradually you dig deeper into the meanings of the Word, and this produces greater challenges as you do so. It also provides a blessing when you discover that some of the previous challenges are now a regular part of your life. Without this kind of record you may not realize that you are growing in grace and knowledge and in wisdom and stature with God.

Daily Spiritual Diary

Week of _____ to_____

"I have esteemed the words of his mouth more than my necessary food" (*Job 23:12*).

Sunday: Passage _____ Date _____

God's message to me today:_____

_____

A Promise from God   A Command to Keep   A Timeless Principle

_____   _____   _____

_____   _____   _____

_____   _____   _____

How does this apply to my life? _____

_____

Monday: Passage_____ Date _____

God's message to me today:_____

_____

A Promise from God   A Command to Keep   A Timeless Principle

_____   _____   _____

_____   _____   _____

_____   _____   _____

How does this apply to my life? _____

_____

Tuesday: Passage_____ Date _____

God's message to me today:_____

_____

A promise from God   A Command to Keep   A Timeless Principle

_____   _____   _____

_____   _____   _____

_____   _____   _____

How does this apply to my life? _____

_____

Additional Comments_____

_____

_____

Daily Spiritual Diary

Wednesday: Passage _____ Date _____

God's message to me today:_____
_____

A Promise from God   A Command to Keep   A Timeless Principle
_____   _____   _____
_____   _____   _____

How does this apply to my life? _____
_____

Thursday: Passage _____ Date _____

God's message to me today:_____
_____

A Promise from God   A Command to Keep   A Timeless Principle
_____   _____   _____
_____   _____   _____

How does this apply to my life? _____
_____

Friday: Passage _____ Date _____

God's message to me today:_____
_____

A Promise from God   A Command to Keep   A Timeless Principle
_____   _____   _____
_____   _____   _____

How does this apply to my life? _____
_____

Saturday: Passage _____ Date _____

God's message to me today:_____
_____

A Promise from God   A Command to Keep   A Timeless Principle
_____   _____   _____
_____   _____   _____

How does this apply to my life? _____
_____

Additional Comments_____

Methods of Bible Reading

There are four recommended methods for reading the Bible.

1.
Read it
by books

The books of the Bible were written either to individuals or to groups of people, and so for that reason they should be read in their entirety. This way you keep in mind the overall message of the book and are less likely to twist a text out of its context.

Some people use the "hunt-and-peck" system. They open the Bible at random and hope they find something for the day. This method is better than nothing, but not much, and sometimes it is dangerous. The story is told of one person using the "hunt-and-peck" method who opened to Matthew 27:5: "And [Judas] went and hanged himself." He then opened to another passage and discovered "Go and do likewise." Still a third "peck" produced the advice, "What thou doest, do quickly."

Such a discovery could be interpreted by the reader as a lack of love on God's part in not providing him better instruction for the day, when in reality it wasn't God's fault but his own disastrous method of Bible reading. This will never happen when you read the Bible by books. It is also advisable to familiarize yourself with the purpose and theme of the book before you begin reading it. This information can usually be located in your Bible or in a copy of *Halley's Bible Handbook.* More will be said about this later.

2.
Read it
repeatedly

One of the best ways to get to know a book of the Bible thoroughly is to read the entire book every day for 30 days. Of course, this method works best for books containing six chapters or less. Most of the epistles can be read this way with great profit. By the thirtieth day you will really know that particular book. However, this method should probably not be used until you have read through the entire New Testament at least once.

3.
Read it
by need

Your personal spiritual needs will often determine what you read, particularly if you read a book repeatedly. If you lack assurance of salvation, I recommend that you read 1 John every day for 30 days. I have yet to find a person plagued by feelings of eternal insecurity after 30 days of reading 1 John, especially if after the tenth day he begins compiling a list of the 27 things that God wants us to know that are found in this little epistle. The entire book can easily be read in approximately 15 minutes. More details will be given on this in the next chapter.

**4.
Read it
entirely**

Every Christian should read the Bible all the way through, beginning with the New Testament. In the next chapter we will discuss this in detail and offer a three-year suggested reading program.

How to Be Consistent in Daily Bible Reading

"Consistency, thou art a gem" is a saying of a friend of mine who all but destroyed himself by inconsistency. However, knowing the problem does not always guarantee a solution. Doubtless more Christians have gone down the spiritual drain or failed to grow in their Christian lives through inconsistency in their daily devotional lives than in any other one thing. As we have seen, it is absolutely essential to get into the Word daily, to keep fresh and filled with the Spirit, but unfortunately, only a small percentage of God's people have found this key.

Self-discipline is not the hallmark of this affluent age in which we live. But it has been my observation that self-discipline is the name of the game as far as success is concerned. Whether it is a Mickey Mantle, whose three to five hours a night as a youngster hitting his father's right-hand pitching and his grandfather's left-hand pitching produced the greatest switch-hitting baseball player of all time, or a Paul Anderson, whose daily hours of weight-lifting made him the strongest man in the world, or Terry Bradshaw, a premier football quarterback, or Billie Jean King, who has won 19 tennis championships at Wimbledon, or Jerry Rice, who has caught more passes than any wide receiver in the history of football, discipline is the name of the game! Admittedly, they also had great talent, as do thousands of other people in this world, but these achievers added the discipline of practice to their talent and thereby became established superstars.

The only difference between my analogy above and the success in the Christian life is that *every* Christian could be a great spiritual success if he would discipline himself to the daily quiet time we have outlined here and the implementation of God's principles into his life. Most of us could never be outstanding athletes because that isn't the area of our talent, but *all* of us can be effective Christians.

If you will pardon a personal illustration, I'll show you what I mean. With over ten million copies in print of my 37 published books, many people have asked why I waited until I was almost 40 years old before writing my first book. The answer is rather humbling, but true: It took me all those years to learn to discipline myself to the work of writing. I used to say, "I'm too busy to write; besides, who would read anything I wrote?" But that wasn't the real problem; I had to finally come to the place, even while I was a busy pastor, that writing was so important to me that it deserved at least one day of my life every week. Now it is no problem for me to be productive.

Until you decide that your spiritual development is worth at least 15 minutes a day in the Word of God, you will remain a mediocre Christian. Remember this: The potential is yours as a gift from God, but what you do with it is up to you.

During the life of our Lord He had various kinds of people who showed an interest in Him. The Bible tells us that "many believed on him," but little is heard of them. Others "came after him," but when persecution and adversity arose they returned home. Still others said, "We would be thy disciples," and He replied, "If any man will come after me, let him *deny himself*, and take up his cross *daily*, and follow me" (Luke 9:23). As is well-known, our Lord had only 12 disciples and another 120 like them who were devoted to the Savior. Isn't it interesting that the words "disciple" and "discipline" are so similar? You can't have the first without the second.

Dr. M.R. DeHaan, the late founder of the nationally aired program "Radio Bible Class," once said, "To come to Christ costs nothing, to follow Christ costs something, but to serve Christ will cost you everything." I would not deceive you: There is a cost involved in spiritual growth and maturity, and that cost is the time it takes to learn God's principles from His Word and the submission of your life to them. However, the rewards and results are well worth the sacrifice they require.

A Guaranteed Formula for Learning Self-Discipline

On the basis of many years spent in helping Christians, particularly men, who wanted to learn discipline in their daily devotional life, I can guarantee the following three-step formula for success. There is no way you can fail if you incorporate these steps.

1.
Read when you feel like it; read when you don't

It would be unrealistic to suggest that every morning when you awake 15 minutes early, your brain will be 100 percent "on" and you will be eager to get into the Word. There will be some mornings like that, but there will also be some when you awake feeling like the rapture occurred and you have been left behind, particularly if you are a late-night worker. But don't give in to the lackadaisical suggestion which your mind offers that "if you don't feel like doing it, you won't get much out of it," or "it's better to wait until you have a hunger for Bible reading," or "you have to be in the right mood to receive a blessing." These are all lies of the devil or our deceitful mind!

If you wake up feeling drowsy or "dead," take a shower and get dressed before your quiet time. But put in your 15 minutes of minimum reading time whether you feel like it or not! Some of the greatest quiet times I have had were when I prayed, "Heavenly Father, I feel lousy this morning, and very honestly I don't even want to read Your Word. Forgive my carnal attitude, and open my mind that I may see wonderful things in your Word today. Amen." Years ago I heard a preacher say, "Read the Word when you feel like it; and when you don't feel like it, read until you do." You will find that as you read your "feeling" will gradually change and you will get a special blessing from His Book.

2. Make a sacred vow with God

Ordinarily I do not challenge Christians to make vows to God, because Scripture says, "It is better not to vow than to vow and not pay" (Ecclesiastes 5:5 NKJV). But since it is so essential to maintain a daily reading of the Word, I make this one exception, because it has a long history of producing the consistency which I believe most Christians desire.

As a young minister I met a missionary whose personal life and consistency I greatly admired. When I asked him for "the secret of your success," he replied, "I never miss a daily time with God in prayer and Bible study." To my question, "How did you learn to be so consistent?" he replied, "Very simple; I made a sacred vow with God: *no Bible, no breakfast*." He then explained that there were a few times in his schedule when he awakened late, or a child was sick, or some emergency prohibited his time in the Word. But when that occurred he said, "I just skip breakfast. If I am too rushed to feed my soul, I am too busy to feed my body. Through the years I've only missed a few breakfasts because of my inability to feed my soul first." I have shared this vow with hundreds of people; many have made and kept it for years.

Recently I told that story during a Bible study in our home for San Diego Charger football players. Two weeks later one of the brilliant special team players told me he had made that vow during our closing prayer and had found it to be a tremendous help in bringing discipline into his spiritual life. Here is an extremely talented young man who had learned to discipline himself athletically, but needed a little mental handle like this to produce discipline in his devotional life.

Very simply, the vow is: *no Bible, no breakfast*. For those who need a Scripture verse to verify everything they do, try Job 23:12: "Neither have I gone back from the commandment of his lips; I have esteemed the words of his mouth more than my necessary food." Evidently Job had his own vow with God that sounds a lot like *no Bible, no breakfast*.

One young athlete who attended our Chargers Bible study wasn't buying my challenge and said, "That wouldn't work for me, since I never eat breakfast anyway." So I replied, "No problem; make your vow *no Bible, no lunch!*" Then I suggested, "Anyone want to try dinner?" The obvious point here is that by tying the feeding of your spiritual person to the feeding of your physical person, you will automatically guarantee sufficient spiritual nutrition to provide for spiritual growth and development.

3.
Make no exceptions

The last part of the formula is very simple: *Make no exceptions*. Once you give in, the vow is broken and it becomes easy to repeat your inconsistency. The refusal to make exceptions is a fundamental requirement to consistency in anything. Alcoholics Anonymous has established for all to know that the only path to victory over the bottle is to *make no exceptions*. "That first drink proved my downfall" is a common wail of the AA member who wound up on skid row again.

Those who diet know this fundamental rule, as do joggers or self-disciplinarians in any field. I remember going three years without touching sweets, during which time I lost 40 pounds. Then I decided I could "handle my sweet tooth now," and took one piece of candy, then another, and gained 15 pounds back before making that vow again. Even now I cannot diet and make exceptions—and neither can you or anyone else.

Right here I would like to issue you a challenge: Try this formula for one year; make your vow, *no Bible, no breakfast*. Allow for no exceptions and you will be a much more consistent and effective Christian in 365 days! Keeping this vow will change your life.

5

What to Read in the Bible

What to read in the Bible is as important as how to read, particularly for a young Christian. When I was a high school student I went to summer youth camp every year. It was there that many of the biggest spiritual decisions of my life were made: surrender of my will to Christ, surrender of my life to the ministry, and many others. I thank God for the people who ran that camp, but I wish they had told me what to read in the Bible.

Each year they would challenge us to read it every day, and each year I would go home from camp determined to be consistent. All through high school I did the same thing: I started at the beginning, as with any other book, and read through Genesis. Fortunately, I enjoy history, so Genesis was a lark, but then came Exodus and the work of Moses. Halfway through that book I got bogged down in the sockets and tapestry of tabernacle construction and gave up, after about two months (that was before I had heard about "no Bible, no breakfast").

It is too bad that someone hadn't told me at that early age that as great as the Old Testament is, it was written largely to Israel and that age, and I am a New Testament Christian. As such I should have learned my way around the New Testament before working on the Old Testament. That should not be taken as an indication that the Old Testament is not important to the Christian; it is, particularly certain books, but it is much more important for Christians to understand the 27 books of the New Testament, for they were written expressly to the church (and the Christians in the church) for their edification.

Everything you need to know about God is found in the Bible. Everything you need to know to grow spiritually strong is found in the Bible. But as the next chapter will show, the Bible is not just an ordinary book; it is a library of 66 books, and just as with any library, you have to go to the right section to get what you need.

The following suggested reading schedule is designed to help streamline the learning process for a young Christian so that he may concentrate on those books that have the answers to his greatest need. If you follow the schedule in this chapter, you will read the most important books for you to know several times the first year, the New Testament through twice, and the entire Bible by the end of the third year. The books are listed in the order that I consider most important. Included is a brief reason why each is so important.

**1.
Read
First John
seven times**

The primary need of every new Christian is the assurance of his salvation. Little spiritual growth is possible until a believer settles the fact that he is an eternal child of God, that what Jesus Christ did on Calvary's cross was to redeem him from all his sins forever and adopt him into the eternal family of God. This truth is so marvelous and so contradictory to human intuition, intelligence, and understanding that it comes *only* through the Word of God. If we waited until we were good enough or "worthy enough" to be assured of eternal life, none of us would have it. The only way to gain that assurance is through the Word of God, and of all the 66 books of the Bible, only the little epistle of First John was written for that express purpose. The author stated his purpose in chapter 5, verse 13, by saying, "These things have I written unto you that believe on the name of the Son of God, that ye may know that ye have eternal life."

Because of First John's unique content and the need of every believer for assurance, you should read this little five-chapter epistle every day for one week, making the appropriate notations in your daily diary. Try not to duplicate any entries that you have used; the book is so full of golden spiritual nuggets that this shouldn't be difficult. If doubts of your salvation persist after seven days, continue in First John seven more days; otherwise move on to reading priority number 2.

**2.
Read the
Gospel of
John twice**

Like your first great need, the increase of your faith in general is vital to an effective Christian life. The best book in the Bible for that is the Gospel of John. The author does not leave us in doubt as to why he wrote the book, for in chapter 20, verses 30 and 31, he stated, "And many other signs truly did Jesus in the presence of his disciples, which are not written in this book: but these are written, that ye might believe that Jesus is the Christ, the Son of God; and that believing ye might have life through his name."

It is said by scholars that the apostle John wrote this Gospel around 85 A.D., long after the other disciples were dead. Matthew, Mark, and Luke had been written some 20 to 25 years earlier, giving a detailed record of our Lord's life, but John lived long enough to hear the teachings of heretics who began challenging the deity of Jesus Christ, suggesting that he was merely a great prophet, teacher, or example, but denying that He was the Son of God. The apostle John, knowing that he was the only remaining eyewitness to the supernatural life of our Lord, set out in the Gospel that bears his name to include those events and teachings that leave no doubt as to the true identity of Jesus Christ. By the time you have read this book twice you will be in a good position to judge how well he accomplished his purpose.

You will find it profitable while reading John's Gospel at the rate of approximately four chapters a day to not only keep your spiritual diary but also to make a list of the seven miracles John recorded that show Christ's supernaturalness. Many Christians have found this book a vital aid to increase their faith. You should be able to read it twice in 11 days, which means that in 18 days you will have read First John seven times and the Gospel of John twice. (If you can't read that fast you should have this goal accomplished in, at most, 25 days.) This means that in less than one month your faith will be well grounded in the Word of God and you will be ready to proceed to other books.

3.
Read the
Gospel of
Mark twice

The Gospel of Mark compresses the life of Christ into 16 short chapters. It is an ideal book for busy people because the author doesn't give a lot of details but covers a host of events in the life of the Savior in a short time. It is extremely important that you read and reread the Gospels, for we are challenged, "Let this mind be in you which was in Christ Jesus," and "As ye have therefore received Christ Jesus the Lord, so walk ye in him." How can we know the mind or walk of Christ unless we know His life? The only way to know that life is to read and reread it in the Gospels. If you are able to maintain the four-chapter-a-day pace, you can read this action-packed Gospel twice in just eight days.

4.
Read the
short epistles
of Paul

Now you are ready for the ten short epistles of Paul: Galatians, Ephesians, Philippians, Colossians, 1 and 2 Thessalonians, 1 and 2 Timothy, Titus, and Philemon. You will find these letters to churches or special Christian friends (Timothy, Titus, and Philemon) to be delightful reading. If possible, try to read the entire epistle in one daily period; however, Galatians, Ephesians, and Timothy may take longer. If you are using a study Bible, you would be wise to read the introductory material at the beginning of the book before you begin reading. As an alternative, read the introduction of the book in *Halley's Bible Handbook.*

5.
Read the Gospel of Luke

Now it will be profitable to return to another of the Gospels of Christ, the book of Luke. This record of His life is the longest and most detailed; you will find things mentioned here that are not included elsewhere.

6.
Read the book of Acts

After completing Luke's Gospel, you will enjoy going right on with the story as Luke tells it in the book of the Acts of the Apostles. You will find it exciting to see how the Holy Spirit used the early Christians as they faithfully witnessed for Him throughout the then-known world.

7.
Read the book of Romans

The best doctrinal book in the New Testament is the book of Romans. Later in our course you should plan a study of the book, but for now a single reading will afford you a bird's-eye view of the wealth of good teaching material found here. One reason this epistle is so unique is that it is probably the only one Paul wrote to a church he had never visited personally. For that reason it is thought to contain many of the concepts which he taught personally when founding a church. Don't be surprised if you find yourself rereading some sections several times. It will probably be difficult for you to read more than three chapters a day, but try not to drop below that figure.

8.
Read
the entire
New
Testament
twice

It will take you 87 days to read the entire New Testament at the rate of three chapters a day. This means it will take you 174 days to read the entire New Testament twice, or almost six months. The previous reading schedule will also take you about six months, meaning that in one year you will have read the entire New Testament twice and the most important parts to young Christians several times. If you have never done this kind of consistent Bible reading before, you will find it to be one of the greatest things you can do for your spiritual life and maturity.

9.
Read the
wisdom
literature of
the Old
Testament

During this first year you will have developed the consistent habit of reading the Word of God at least 15 minutes a day. In the process you will have developed an overall picture of the New Testament and will now be ready for key sections of the Old Testament. Incidentally, this first year will also have made your attendance at a Bible-teaching church much more enjoyable and you will no doubt be enjoying your pastor's sermons more because you will have a better understanding of how his messages relate to the whole of the New Testament. (This understanding will increase as you proceed into the Old Testament.)

The wisdom literature of the Old Testament contains most of the timeless principles of God that have been a stabilizing influence on the people of God for over 3000 years. The wisdom books include Job, Psalms, Proverbs, Ecclesiastes, and the Song of Solomon. But rather than have you read them in that order, I would like to suggest a more helpful sequence.

First of all, begin this foray into the Old Testament wisdom literature by developing the habit of reading one chapter in the book of Proverbs daily. In my opinion, this is the most important book in the Old Testament except for the book of Genesis, which explains man's origins. The reason I say that is because Proverbs contains more timeless principles to live by than any other book in the Bible. Its author was endowed with two blessings: He was raised by a devoted, godly father who taught him the commandments, statutes, and proverbs of the godly men before him, and he was endowed by God with the unique gift of wisdom.

In fact, Scripture says of Solomon, "Before him there was none greater, neither would there be after him." "And God gave Solomon wisdom and exceedingly great understanding, and largeness of heart like the sand on the seashore. Thus Solomon's wisdom excelled the wisdom of all the men of the East and all the wisdom of Egypt. For he was wiser than all men. . .and his fame was in all the surrounding nations" (1 Kings 4:29-31 NKJV). I believe the book of Proverbs contains the basic principles that God wants you to obey in order to be happy and productive. He even promises that keeping them will lengthen your life (Proverbs 9:10,11).

The book of Proverbs lends itself to daily reading by virtue of the fact that it has 31 chapters. If you start on the first day of the month you can develop the habit of reading the chapter that coincides with the calendar. By doubling up one day on the 30-day months you will stay in sequence. Many businessmen find such reading in Proverbs to be one of the most helpful things they can do to prepare themselves for the daily rigors of the business world.

Since there are 212 chapters in Job, Psalms, Ecclesiastes, and Song of Solomon, you will find that in less than four months—by reading one chapter daily of Proverbs and two chapters daily of the other wisdom books— you will have read them through once and Proverbs four times. To fill in the remaining 32 chapters (because this actually takes 3½ months), check the Psalms you enjoyed most as you read them and then go back and reread the 30 you liked best along with your Proverbs chapter each day.

10.
Read
selected
books
repeatedly

Once having digested the wisdom books, it is time to return to key New Testament books to read repeatedly as previously suggested (every day for 30 days). This method of Bible reading is extremely beneficial not only in developing a rather thorough knowledge of that book but also in helping its concepts become a part of you. It may be that you will find other short books you wish to read repeatedly other than those I suggest. After reading my reasons for selecting certain books, if you feel your book choices are more beneficial for your needs, feel free to make substitutions. Since there are eight months left in your second reading year, I make the following suggestions.

First John

I recommend First John for the reasons already given, primarily for the bolstering of your faith and your assurance of salvation. However, there are also other valuable teachings in this five-chapter epistle, such as forgiveness, love of the brethren, testing spiritual teachers, guidance, prayer, and much more.

Ephesians

The six chapters of Ephesians make it the longest in the group of suggested books, but it is exceedingly practical. Ephesians not only deals with the special blessings we receive in this church age, but it also reveals the challenge to a spiritual walk in detail, it shows the cure for anger, it contains the most specific command in the Bible on being filled with the Holy Spirit, it has the most complete instructions on family living in the New Testament, and it sums this all up with a challenge to put on our spiritual armor so that we can stand against the devilish temptations of the adversary. Any Christian, no matter what his spiritual level of maturity, could profit from the reading of this great book every day for one month.

Philippians   The epistle of joy which Paul sent from a prison cell to the church of Philippi is a call to joyous Christian living. It lifts our spirits and challenges us more than any other book to a consistent walk above the circumstances of life rather than defeat below them. I have assigned the daily reading of this book to many sad and despondent Christians with quite remarkable success.

Colossians   This little epistle is a condensed version of several of Paul's writings; it is like drinking spiritual cream for the soul. You can find a new challenge every day for a month and still not exhaust its treasures.

First Thessalonians   Paul was in the city of Thessalonica only about three weeks, yet he clearly taught the believers the Christian doctrine of resurrection from the dead and the second coming of Christ. In fact, he mentions the coming of the Lord in every chapter.

James   This five-chapter epistle is the balance wheel to the Christian life. It puts the life of faith in proper perspective by making it the motivation for faith. No Christian is prepared to serve God who is not familiar with the challenge to possess a faith that is demonstrated by works.

Romans 5–8   The heart of the teaching section of Romans is chapters 5–8, so try to read all four of these chapters each day for a month so you can get a basic understanding of them and their relationship to each other. In short, they cover justification by faith, the worthlessness of the flesh, and our dependence on the Holy Spirit for victory in the Christian life.

John 14-17   As our Lord prepared to leave His disciples to carry on the work He had trained them for, He compressed some vital teachings they needed to know into the last few hours He had with them before His trial and crucifixion. These four chapters contain the gist of those important teachings. Every Christian should master them, and for this reason they too are included in the schedule of repeated readings of important chapters and books.

If you follow this schedule carefully, you will have been reading your Bible daily with great profit for two full years. Now you are ready to . . .

There are 1190 chapters in the Bible, 929 in the Old Testament and 261 in the New Testament. If you read three chapters a day and five on Sunday, you can read the entire Bible in 362 days. Many Christians read it through this way every year. One of the greatest Bible teachers I ever heard was the late Dr. Harry Ironside, who at 72 years of age had read the Bible through each year of his life. Near the end of his life he went blind, but he kept right on preaching because he knew most of the Bible by heart.

Since there are only 261 chapters in the New Testament, I suggest that you read one chapter from the New Testament each of six days of the week plus two from the Old Testament. On the 313th day of the year you will have finished the New Testament and should concentrate on the Old until it is finished. Through this painless but regular procedure, in three years you will have worked your way through the whole Bible once, the whole New Testament three times, the wisdom literature twice, and many of the most important chapters and books several times. No matter how new a Christian you are when you start, if you will keep up your spiritual diary as suggested, you will no longer be a baby Christian after this three-year program.

The Three-Year Bible-Reading Schedule

First Year

Read...   First John seven times
John twice
Mark twice
Galatians through Philemon
Luke
Acts
Romans
The New Testament twice.

Second Year

Read...   A proverb every day for four months
Two other wisdom literature chapters daily
(Job, Psalms, Ecclesiastes, Song of Solomon).
Read repeatedly for one month the following:
First John
Ephesians
Philippians
First Thessalonians
James
Romans 5-8
John 14-17

Third Year

Read...   One New Testament chapter daily
Two Old Testament chapters daily
Five Old Testament chapters each Sunday.

The Bible: The World's Greatest Library

The Bible is the most unique book ever written, for three reasons: One, it was written by a loving God to sinful man to instruct him in matters of both God and man; two, it is not just one book, but a library of 66 books; and three, it is the only book in the world that tells man the truth about the past, present, and future. Consequently, it is not necessary to spend time proving its truth. You will, however, find it helpful to know something about how the Bible came into being and why.

The word "Bible" comes from the Greek word "biblion," which means "book." When we think of a book we picture a hardback or well-bound paperback book that can stand upright on a shelf. But ancient books were written on papyrus reed and were made in the form of scrolls.

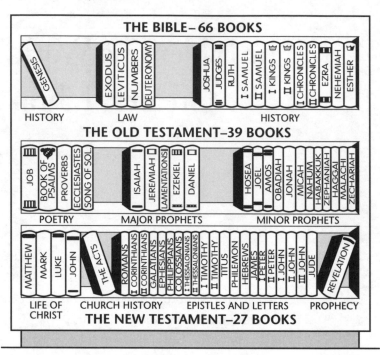

God's Three Revelations

There are three specific ways that God has revealed Himself to mankind.

1.
Through
creation

Psalm 19:1 says, "The heavens declare the glory of God, and the firmament showeth his handiwork." Romans 1:19,20 states, "Because that which may be known of God is manifest in them, for God hath showed it unto them. For the invisible things of him from the creation of the world are clearly seen, being understood by the things that are made, even his eternal power and Godhead, so that they are without excuse."

These and other Scriptures clearly indicate that God has given ample evidence in creation that He exists. There are serious limitations to that form of revelation, however, for we do not learn a great deal about God's personal nature and nothing about His grace, love, and mercy for man.

2.
Through
Jesus Christ

God has given a more specific revelation of Himself to man. Hebrews 1:1-3 says, "God, who at sundry times and in diverse manners spoke in time past unto the fathers by the prophets, hath in these last days spoken unto us by his Son, whom he hath appointed heir of all things, by whom also he made the worlds; who being the brightness of his glory and the express image of his person, and upholding all things by the word of his power, when he had by himself purged our sins, sat down on the right hand of the Majesty on high." Jesus Christ revealed God to man in everything He did; that's why if you want to know about God, then study the life of Christ. All man really needs to know about God is found in the Person of the Lord Jesus Christ.

But unless you happened to live during the time of His life, you would never have known about that revelation of God were it not for the Bible.

3.
Through
the Bible
Of the three revelations of God, the 66 books of the Bible provide us the most complete revelation information about Him, and because the Bible is permanently in our grasp, we can study at our own discretion. God has promised to illuminate us through His Spirit as we carefully read and study this third revelation. The diagram describes the process and end result of God's revelation, the Bible.

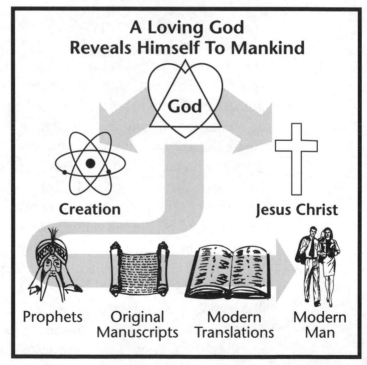

A Loving God
Reveals Himself To Mankind

God

Creation

Jesus Christ

Prophets

Original Manuscripts

Modern Translations

Modern Man

The Organization of the Bible

One of the incredible things about the Bible is its amazing organization. No book of man could possibly have been written that way, for it was not compiled by a single author within a particular lifetime, but was written by over 40 different people during a period of 1600 years, yet it shows the unmistakable hand of one overall mind. That can be accounted for only on the basis of God revealing Himself to these men during their various lifetimes. Most of them never knew the others and many were not aware that others were even writing. Yet when put together the 66 books in the library of God make one composite whole.

The reason for this unity and wholeness of design is not difficult to understand when you keep in mind that these men knew they were not speaking for themselves but that God spoke through them. Consider the testimony of these writers:

Moses: "And God said unto Moses, I AM THAT I AM; and he said, Thus shalt thou say unto the children of Israel: I AM hath sent me unto you" (Exodus 3:14).

Joshua: "Now after the death of Moses the servant of the Lord it came to pass that the Lord spoke unto Joshua the son of Nun, Moses' minister, saying . . . " (Joshua 1:1).

Samuel: "And the Lord said to Samuel, Behold, I will do a thing in Israel at which both the ears of everyone that heareth it shall tingle" (1 Samuel 3:11).

David: "The Spirit of the Lord spoke by me, and his word was in my tongue" (2 Samuel 23:2).

Jeremiah: "The word of the Lord came also unto me, saying . . . For thus saith the Lord, enter not into the house of mourning, neither go to lament nor bemoan them; for I have taken away my peace from this people, saith the Lord, even lovingkindness and mercies. . . . For thus saith the Lord of hosts, the God of Israel, Behold, I will cause to cease out of this place in your eyes, and in your days, the voice of mirth and the voice of gladness, the voice of the bridegroom and the voice of the bride. . . . Therefore, behold, the days come, saith the Lord, that it shall no more be said, The Lord liveth, who brought up the children of Israel out of the land of Egypt" (Jeremiah 16:1,5,9,14).

The 39 books of the Old Testament were written in Hebrew by at least 32 different men, from a variety of educational and vocational backgrounds, including priests, prophets, judges, kings, and shepherds, and covering a time period of approximately 1600 years. One of the first things you should do in the study of the Word is to memorize the books of the Bible by divisions. This will help you find your way around in the Scriptures when discussing the Word or hearing it taught, and it will better enable you to compare Scripture with Scripture.

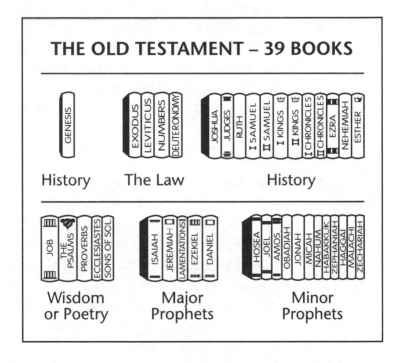

THE OLD TESTAMENT – 39 BOOKS

History | The Law | History

Wisdom or Poetry | Major Prophets | Minor Prophets

The divisions of the Bible were not written in this exact order but have been arranged in these groups for the sake of convenience. The

Jews have only 22 books in their Scriptures, for they combine such books as 1 and 2 Kings, Ezra, Nehemiah, Esther, and others, but the content is essentially the same as our 39 books of the Old Testament.

In the New Testament there is repeated reference to Moses and the prophets. This twofold grouping places the five books of Moses, which we call "the law" division, in one group and then places all the rest into another, called "the prophets," because in a sense all the writers were prophets or spokesmen for God. You will find that the five divisions make it much easier to remember how each book relates to the whole. The following descriptions will help you become acquainted with each division.

1.
The Law

These books are sometimes called the "Pentateuch" or the five books of Moses. The Jews call them "the Torah," meaning "the law." They consider them on a higher level of inspiration than the other Old Testament books; we do not. The first six chapters of Genesis contain some of the most sublime literature in all the world dealing with creation, man's origin, the fall, and the conditions that led to the worldwide flood. Obviously God did not reveal everything to us about that period of about 1600 years from Adam to Noah, for it is all condensed into six chapters. This is in stark contrast to the other 923 chapters, which cover a period of only about 2000 years in the history of Israel from Noah to Malachi. The stories of many men of God are recorded in the Pentateuch, including those of Abraham, Isaac, Jacob, Joseph, Moses, and many others.

Included in these books are the history of mankind, the development of Israel as the "chosen people," their 40 years of wandering in the wilderness, and the giving of the law and God's special instruction to them as a people. These ancient books are among the oldest known to mankind and have teachings that are singularly unique. They defy human primitive concepts and standards but were written on such a sublime level that they are still unsurpassed as literature, just as you would expect if they were really authored by God.

2. History

The next 12 books found in your Bible cover about 1100 years, from the entering into the Promised Land under the leadership of Joshua to the partial restoration back into the land after the Babylonian captivity. You will find the exciting stories of judges like Gideon and Samson, kings like Saul, David, Solomon, and many others. In a real way, this history is the fulfilling of God's prophecy to Israel in Deuteronomy 28 that if they would obey Him He would bless them, but that if they disobeyed Him He would curse them. As clearly seen in these books of history, the times of Israel's blessings followed their obedience to God, while their periods of national disgrace and sorrow followed their times of disobedience.

One of the things you will enjoy in these books is the characters that God raised up at key periods of history. It shows us that He is willing to use imperfect human beings and is faithful to the person who obeys Him. We are challenged in the New Testament to read these dealings of God with His people because they are examples of how He wants to work in our lives today.

3.
Wisdom
and Poetry

We have already examined the importance of learning the wisdom literature of the Bible, so we shall not repeat it. But these timeless principles show how to enjoy success and blessing regardless of the political and religious circumstances into which a person is born. Some Bible teachers call these "the books of poetry" because they were largely written as poetry, particularly Psalms and Proverbs. That is why the writers sometimes say almost the same thing in the last half of a verse as they did in the first. This is called "Hebrew parallelism" and usually adds further insight into the original statement. Once you get used to this style you will enjoy it. I have met many people who read one Psalm and one chapter of Proverbs each day.

Care should be taken in reading the other three books. Job contains some bad advice that should not be taken as God's truth but as man's philosophical attempt to explain tragedy without God's insights (see Job 42:7, 8). If you keep the overall story in view, you will have no problem.

Ecclesiastes is a different matter; it contains the frustrations of Solomon at the end of his life, after turning his back on God and disobeying the principles of God that he well knew. Never build your life on the humanistic conclusions of this backslidden king, unless it is to recognize the futility of man apart from God.

The Song of Solomon contains the intimate story of the beauties of married love. It shows that God designed sex for married pleasure and love.

**4.
Major
Prophets**

The four prophets who wrote the five books called "major prophets" were the outstanding prophets in the entire history of Israel. Isaiah called the nation of Judah to repentance, which saved the country from the judgment of God for another 130 years. Jeremiah tried the same thing in his day but was rejected.

His little book of Lamentations is his sad lament that the great city of Jerusalem and the nation of Judah were unnecessarily destroyed because they rejected the Lord. Ezekiel and Daniel were taken captive into Babylon and prophesied the restoration of Israel prior to the first coming of Christ and again in the "last days." Daniel's prophecy is considered outstanding in the Old Testament and is comparable to the book of Revelation in the New Testament.

**5.
Minor
Prophets**

The 12 minor prophets were raised up by God at strategic times in the history of Israel to call the people back to God. They are called "minor" prophets because their books are shorter. Although these books are limited largely to the people to whom they were written, there are many blessings to be found hidden in these prophecies.

The Silent Years

From the close of the Old Testament to the birth of Christ, over 400 years transpired when Israel had no prophet to reveal the message of God. For that reason these are called "silent years." They were completed with the coming of the prophet John the Baptist.

The 27 books of the New Testament were written in Greek by eight men, three of whom (Matthew, John, and Peter) were apostles and eyewitnesses of what they wrote about Christ. Luke was a constant traveling companion of Paul and thus saw many of the events he wrote about in Acts. He researched the events in the life of Christ in order to write the Gospel that bears his name. Luke is a presentation of the life of Christ as testified to by the very people who saw the events recorded. The other Gospel writers told what they had seen personally.

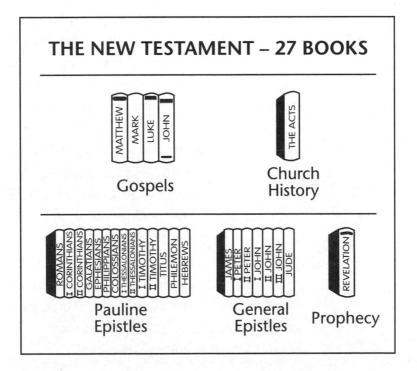

THE NEW TESTAMENT – 27 BOOKS

Gospels
— MATTHEW, MARK, LUKE, JOHN

Church History
— THE ACTS

Pauline Epistles
— ROMANS, I CORINTHIANS, II CORINTHIANS, GALATIANS, EPHESIANS, PHILIPPIANS, COLOSSIANS, I THESSALONIANS, II THESSALONIANS, I TIMOTHY, II TIMOTHY, TITUS, PHILEMON, HEBREWS

General Epistles
— JAMES, I PETER, II PETER, I JOHN, II JOHN, III JOHN, JUDE

Prophecy
— REVELATION

The first New Testament book written was James, in about 50 A.D., and the last one was Revelation, written about 96 A.D., approximately 46 years later. However, the events these two books describe covered a period of time close to a hundred years, from the birth of Christ to John's vision of revelation on the Isle of Patmos. I urge you to memorize the names of these 27 books by their divisions so you can better familiarize yourself with the whole library of God.

1. The Gospels

The New Testament begins with the four histories of the life of Christ, called the Gospels. Everything that can be known about the life of Jesus Christ is found in these four books, and for that reason it is of paramount importance that you read and reread them. No one of the Gospels is complete in itself. Some events of our Lord's life are included in all four, but each presents Him in a slightly different light, depending on to whom it was written and the purpose of its writing. To know Christ's entire life you must familiarize yourself with all four of the Gospels. By reading three chapters a day you can read all four Gospels in one month (that would be a good reading exercise for the first six months of your fourth reading year).

**2.
Church
History**

The 28 chapters of the book of Acts contain the only authentic record of the exciting spread of Christianity after the ascension of Christ. It is labeled the Acts of the Apostles, but it could well be called "the acts of the Holy Spirit," for His hand is vitally present throughout the book.

Written by Luke, a Greek medical doctor, this book shows meticulous scholarship. So many geographical places are mentioned that several skeptics set out to disprove Luke's authenticity by visiting them, only to be overcome with the book's painstaking accuracy.

**3.
The
Pauline
Epistles**

The largest division of the New Testament is the 13 Pauline epistles. Each one was written to a church or person for some special purpose. Paul, "the apostle born out of due time," was the intrepid missionary of the early church who did more to spread Christianity than any man on record. His dramatic conversion is a classic illustration of the power of Christ to change lives, for he turned from being a Christ-hating Pharisee to a Christ-serving Christian. Almost every human need is covered in one or another of his epistles.

4.
The
General
Epistles

These are so designated because they were written individually for a specific need or to a group not reached by Paul. They cover a general area of truth needed by God's people of every age. Do not make the mistake of assuming that our lack of description of each book in this division indicates they are not important, for they are literally filled with God's truth needed by today's Christians.

5.
Prophecy

The last book in the library of God is very fittingly the greatest prophecy in the Bible, called Revelation. It is a revelation of our Lord during three stages of history: 1) the church age; 2) the coming tribulation period, culminating with the second coming of Christ; and 3) the new order, which consists of the thousand-year kingdom of Christ on this earth and the final replacement of this earth with a better and eternal one called "the new heavens and the new earth."

This book is often considered the most exciting in the Bible, but admittedly it is more difficult to understand than the others. Don't be surprised if there is much about it that you do not grasp by simple reading; this book has to be studied carefully in the light of many other passages of Scripture. However, there is ample material in it that you can understand and from which you will receive spiritual inspiration to warrant your reading it frequently. (As an aid to understanding the more difficult sections, see the author's commentary on the book, *Revelation—Illustrated and Made Plain,* published by Zondervan Publishing House.)

We have now briefly described the organization of the whole library of God as it appears today. You will find it a fascinating and inexhaustible library to study. It is the only book that is able to "make thee wise unto salvation . . . " (2 Timothy 3:15).

7

How to Study the Bible by Books

We have already seen that reading is the foundation of all Bible study. Next to reading comes writing, for both are an aid to memory and provide a handy source of reference and review in later days; that is why we advocate developing your own personal Bible study notebook. The first section should contain your personal daily diary. After that should come the various methods of Bible studies that will be suggested in this chapter.

The simple devotional reading already discussed that is essential for daily spiritual growth is the easiest form of Bible study. I list it separately because it is, in my opinion, the very minimum spiritual food required to keep a Christian growing, but it is not enough to make him a strong *workman* for God. The theme verse of this book tells it very well: "Study to show thyself approved unto God, a workman that needeth not to be ashamed, rightly dividing the word of truth" (2 Timothy 2:15).

The key words in this verse are *approved* and *workman*. It is possible to be a Christian without any personal effort because salvation is a free gift of God. But if you are ever going to be an "approved workman" for God you will have to study the Bible. That shouldn't take you by surprise, for the same thing is true of anything today. To be a carpenter, plumber, plasterer, or electrician you must study and serve as an apprentice for three to four years before becoming a journeyman or approved workman. Whether it is the construction field or the professions, all competent work takes study. You are no doubt well aware that as a general rule, the highest-paid professionals today—lawyers, doctors, architects, and psychiatrists—require the greatest amount of training and experience. The poorest-paid jobs require the least preparation.

Recently I had the very sad experience of informing a 44-year-old father of four that his job was being phased out and there was no other position in our organization that paid enough to support his family. What a waste! He was halfway through life but totally untrained for any kind of work. As he left my office, I was reminded that the church is filled with many people just like him—spiritually unprepared for any kind of Christian service simply because they are unskilled in the Word of God. Not only will this be reflected at the judgment seat of Christ when their bank account in heaven is examined, but it also keeps them from enjoying the maximum blessing in this life, which comes in serving Christ in whatever way He directs. The saddest part of it all is that it is entirely unnecessary; anyone with a real desire to serve God today can do so—if he is willing to study the Word of God.

Three things are required to successfully study the Word of God: *mental work, discipline, and time.* If you put those three ingredients together, you can be a "workman approved unto God."

1. Mental Work

This book will help you in the "mental work" ingredient by making helpful suggestions on what to do and provide you with various charts to spark your thinking. This will keep you from floundering around in confusion and make it possible to get maximum training out of the time you have available for Bible study.

**2.
Discipline**

You are the only person who can produce self-discipline in your life. It has long been my observation that discipline is the key to success in any field. That is why some young people who have graduated from Bible college fail in life; they have never learned to discipline themselves while in school. They may have studied to pass tests and qualify for graduation, but they were never consistent in the daily study of the Word; consequently, they learned little or nothing of the Word after graduation. I suggest that you set a disciplined minimum requirement on study just as you did for reading—otherwise it will just become a good intention that never materializes.

**3.
Time**

The minimum time allotment for study should be 15 minutes a day *in addition to reading!* For convenience' sake this may be divided into three 30-minute segments a week, or else just lengthen your daily reading quiet time to 30 minutes, with the last 15 minutes being reserved for study. The only danger to this is that you might be tempted to run your reading time over into your study time and omit the study. For that reason it is best to have your devotional reading and Bible study scheduled at different times.

Many working men and women prefer to have their devotional time before going to work and reserve their Bible study for evenings. Housewives and mothers often prefer to wait until the family leaves for work and school and do both on a 30-minute basis. Still others prefer to do their Bible study during their children's afternoon naptime. *When* you have it is really not so important. *That* you have it is!

One of the best illustrations of this principle was a 34-year-old welder with an eighth-grade education whom I had the joy of leading to Christ. It turned out that his godly mother had been praying daily for his conversion for 27 years. When he was one month old in Christ he visited her and went to her little church. It just so happened that his sister was the Sunday school superintendent; she asked him to give his testimony, which he did reluctantly. It took all of one minute and 30 seconds! I have never seen a man with a hunger to study the Word of God like he had. It was largely for him that I worked out the study program in this chapter, which he followed consistently.

Nine months later he visited his family again, and his sister asked him to deliver a Bible study during the Sunday school hour, to which he gladly agreed. The entire congregation was amazed to see this ten-month-old "babe in Christ" deliver a well-thought-out

40-minute message. Afterward the young minister of the church asked him, "what in the world have you been doing to learn the Bible that fast? I've never seen anyone grow like this before."

I watched that man go on to become an effective Bible teacher and soulwinner who has held almost every office in his church. The secret was mental work, plus self-discipline, plus time spent in the study of the Word. In his case it equaled rapid spiritual growth and usability as a "workman approved unto God." And it will work in your case also if you follow the same procedure.

Priorities of Bible Study

Just saying "study the Bible" can scare some people, for they don't know how to go about it. We will now consider seven of the best methods, and I would like to list them in the order of their greatest importance; it is my suggestion that you follow in the order listed, beginning primarily with number 2.

**1.
Study the
Bible as a
whole**
We have already seen that the Bible is a library of 66 books, each written for a specific purpose yet with an overall consistent message from God to man. It is important that you

have an overall picture of the whole Word of God so that each of the other methods listed here can be studied in the light of the whole. You will find that the overall concept will naturally result from the three-year reading program which we have outlined in the preceding chapter.

2.
Study the
Bible
by books

The heart of a Bible study program is to study it as it was written—by individual books. As we have seen, each book was written to a church, a group of people, or an individual. Most of the books were written as letters, and the author may not have known it was going to be a timeless message that would be studied by millions. But God, of course, knew this, and He was also aware that the basic problems, teachings, and meanings would be just as relevant after 2000 years as they were in the day they were written.

Choosing the Right Book to Study

It is very important that you select the right book to study, particularly in the early days of your program, for if you make a faulty selection you may get discouraged. The following suggestions should help in your selection.

1.
Choose a book

It is obviously much more difficult to get an overall picture of the 28 chapters of Acts or Matthew than the four chapters of Philippians or Colossians.

2.
Select an easy book

2. Select an easy book. Admittedly, some books of the Bible are easier to understand than others. For example, Revelation, 1 Peter, Hebrews, and Romans are much more complex than 1 John, 1 Thessalonians, or the Gospel of John; therefore it is not advisable to start with them. Many of the questions that arise in these more difficult books will be more easily answered *after* you have studied some of the easier ones.

3.
Select a "today" book

Start with a book that is highly practical for today, one from which you can benefit spiritually as you study. All Scripture is profitable, but some is more profitable than others for your current needs, particularly at different stages of your Christian life. The same list we suggested for reading would be a good guide to follow (see Chapter 5).

Repeated Reading

After selecting the right book to read, it is important for you to work on mastering the contents of the book. If you enjoy reading that is not too difficult, all you have to do is read the book repeatedly, perhaps ten or twelve times in one sitting. That, of course, will take longer than we originally suggested, but if you give three to four hours to doing this sometime you will be amazed at how much it will mean to you and how much you will get out of it.

If you begin your study of a book after you have read and reread a book in your quiet time, as previously suggested, you will find this extremely helpful also. Only after repeated readings will you begin to see the book "fall into place" in your mind, or see the various strains and fascinating lines of thought that run through it.

Basic Questions to Ask

Once you have read the book at least a dozen times, you are ready to begin answering some basic questions that will further help you to grasp the total message of the book. The following list is prepared for that purpose:

1. Author?
2. What were the circumstances of the author when writing?
3. To whom was the book written?
4. Tell something about them.

5. Where written?
6. When written?
7. Why written?
8. What were the major problems?
9. What solutions were given?
10. What was the central meaning in that day?
11. What is the central meaning today?

Additional comments:

Refer to the accompanying sample book-study chart (pages 97-98), which is designed to fit into a medium-sized notebook. Although it is copyrighted, you are at liberty to make copies for your own personal use (copies for resale are not permitted). Several additional copies are included in the last chapter. Feel free to have additional copies printed as you desire. You will find this questionnaire a handy guide in this phase of your Bible study. When completed, it will provide an excellent source of review in the years to come.

Outlining the Book

Once you have answered the above questions, you are ready to outline the book. To do so, you should have read it through sufficiently often that the main theme or purpose of the book stands out clearly to you. Reduce that theme to a single sentence and write it in the space provided on your Bible study outline form. Then select one or two verses that provide the key to the whole book and list them in the appropriate place.

As you prepare your outline, you would be wise to use scratch paper because you may decide to change your wordings upon subsequent readings. Pick out the major topics, usually three to five points in the smaller books. Don't be deceived by the chapter divisions in your Bible. They were not done by the original authors; in fact, they didn't appear until the fourteenth century and were done rather hurriedly. You will find that sometimes two or three chapters cover a single subject; for example, 1 Corinthians chapters 12, 13, and 14 cover spiritual gifts.

After you have settled on the main divisions of your outline, write them on the chart but leave room for subpoints to be inserted later. It is best to cite the verses for each major and minor division in your outline.

Whenever possible, try to coordinate your study of the Bible by books with the program previously mentioned on reading a book through every day for 30 days. Not only will you have read it over 30 times devotionally, but you will have studied it until you have a working knowledge of the book, so that with only occasional reviews of your notes you should be able to remember most of its teaching for life.

Book Study

Book _____ Date _____

Summarize the main theme: _____
_____
_____
_____

Pick a key verse: _____
_____
_____
_____

Outline: _____
_____
_____
_____
_____
_____
_____
_____
_____
_____
_____
_____
_____
_____
_____
_____
_____

Book Study

Name of Book _____ **How Many Times Read?** ___

Date _____

1. Author: _____

2. What were the circumstances of the author when writing? _____
_____

3. To whom was the book written? _____

4. Tell something about them: _____
_____
_____

5. Where written? _____

6. When written? _____

7. Why written? _____
_____

8. What were the major problems? _____
_____
_____
_____

9. What solutions were given? _____
_____
_____
_____

10. What was the central meaning in that day? _____
_____
_____
_____

11. What is the central meaning today? _____
_____
_____
_____

12. Additional comments: _____
_____
_____

How to Study the Bible by Chapters

Next to book studies, you will probably enjoy chapter analysis as much as any other kind of study. One advantage is that it is usually brief enough so that you can keep the central thoughts in mind. The most ideal division of any Bible study is the chapter, because of the length and content of chapters. The average chapter is about 25 verses, a handy length to read, and although chapters are often divided into several paragraphs, they usually have one central lesson or subject. You will find them a handy length to work with and chapter analysis a rich source of blessing.

The Twelve Chapters to Master

All chapters of the Bible are not equally rich to believers of this age, but hundreds from among the 1189 chapters prove invaluable for personal study. The following 12 chapters are, in my opinion, the most important for Christians to master and are listed in the order I consider them most significant (Group A). If you will analyze these 12 first, spending no more than one week on each, you will no doubt find others from among your daily readings which you will wish to analyze. In Group B you will find some of my additional suggestions in case you do not find your own chapters.

Group A
Ephesians 5
Galatians 5
John 14-17
Romans 6, 8, 12
1 Timothy 2
Ephesians 4, 6

Group B
John 1, 3-5
Matthew 5-7, 13, 24,25
Matthew 26-28
John 11, 12, 18-21
Acts 2, 3
1 Corinthians 6, 15
2 Corinthians 4-6
Proverbs 3
Psalms 1, 27, 37

How to Analyze a Chapter

All of the Bible is profitable. Some passages, however, are more so than others. Like almost any book, you should read some chapters once or twice, but others more frequently until they become a part of you. Some chapters should be read so you can see where they fit into the whole library of God; others should be analyzed until they are mastered.

Analyzing a chapter is not difficult, but it does take time. Read the chapter through at least ten times. By that time you will begin to see the real purpose of the passage. The following questions will further aid you in understanding the chapter.

1. What is the main subject?
2. Who are the main people?
3. What does it say about Christ?
4. What is the key or main verse?
5. What is the central lesson?
6. What are the main promises?
7. What are the main commands?
8. What error should I avoid?
9. What example is here?
10. What do I need most in this chapter to apply to my life today?

Refer to the accompanying notebook-size chart to help make this chapter analysis.

Chapter Analysis

Passage_____ **Date** _____

1. What is the main subject?_____
_____
_____
_____

2. Who are the main people? _____
_____
_____

3. What does it say about Christ? _____
_____
_____
_____

4. What is the key or main verse?_____
_____
_____

5. What is the central lesson? _____
_____
_____

6. What are the main promises? _____
_____
_____

7. What are the main commands?_____
_____
_____

8. What error should I avoid? _____
_____
_____

9. What example is here? _____
_____
_____

10. What do I need most in this chapter to apply to my life today? _____
_____
_____

Chapter Outline

Chapter _____ **Date** _____

Summarize the main subject: _____

_____

_____

_____

_____

_____

_____

_____

_____

_____

Select the key verse: _____

_____

_____

Outline: _____

_____

_____

_____

_____

_____

_____

_____

_____

_____

_____

_____

_____

_____

_____

_____

Additional charts will be found in the back of the book.

Summarizing the Chapter

Once the above ten questions are completed, you should proceed to make your own summary of the chapter. By this time you should know it so well that you can reduce the entire chapter to a three- to five-line paragraph. When that is completed, you are ready to make an outline of the chapter.

Outlining the Chapter

Most good translations have simplified the process of outlining a chapter because they have separated them into paragraphs. The New Scofield Bible with the updated King James Version has a little paragraph symbol which is used to designate distinct changes of subject within a chapter. You will find that paragraph analysis (the detailed breaking down of a section into its main points) can be done to great profit.

Sometimes you will find that your chapter divisions are different from the publisher's. Remember, the Bible was not originally written with any punctuation or paragraphing, so your divisions are as good as anyone's. If you use the New Scofield Bible, don't become enslaved to its paragraph or subparagraph headings. Many Bible students prefer the New American Standard Bible, partly for its modern phrasing but also because, although it is divided into chapters, it does not have as many inserted titles. In either case, you should strive for originality. Outlining is quite simple once you have picked out the key paragraphs; they then become your main points. Once these are established, you can concentrate on the subpoints.

Within your paragraph should be two other smaller divisions that many students of Scripture like to examine carefully. One is verse analysis. The Bible has many outstanding verses that are worthy of study and will provide great inspiration and spiritual blessing. The other division is word studies, in which you trace a word back to its original meaning by using a Greek or Hebrew dictionary (in a later chapter we will describe how even those who have never taken Greek or Hebrew can do that profitably), then find the first time the word is used, then begin there and trace it through the Scriptures. There are over 6000 English words used in our modern Bible; obviously you will never run out of subject matter!

When your chapter analysis sheet has been carefully completed, place it in your notebook in a special chapter section. By rereading it for review from time to time, it will help the basic truth of this chapter to sink firmly into your mind. Years of classroom teaching has convinced me that review is essential to most memories. One of the dangers of an education is that once a student has taken his final exam, he is apt to forget most of what he learned. Periodic reviews will help considerably in the retention of the material you have learned. The mind is a marvelous conditioning mechanism, and the best conditioning in the world is to "renew your mind" with the Word of God. That's why we have it!

Other Study Procedures

There are many other methods of Bible study.

Repeated Readings

We have already seen that reading is at the heart of all learning, and the best reading method is every day for 15 to 30 minutes. The same thing applies for a single chapter, except that you should read it over ten to twelve times before attempting an analysis. One thing you can do that will really make the chapter come to life is underline the verbs. The action of a passage is shown in its verbs; after underlining them, you can easily see the flow of a passage by going back and studying the verbs. Consider the following passage in Romans 6:11-13:

> Likewise *reckon* ye also yourselves to be dead indeed unto sin but alive unto God through Jesus Christ our Lord. *Let* not sin therefore *reign* in your mortal body, that ye should *obey* it in the lusts thereof. Neither *yield* ye your members as instruments of unrighteousness unto sin, but *yield* yourselves unto God as those that are alive from the dead, and your members as instruments of righteousness unto God.

Character Studies

Some of the most interesting people who have ever lived walk through the Bible with a heavy foot. Someone has said there are approximately 2930 different men and women in the Old and New Testaments. Admittedly, some are only referred to once or twice, but others were key figures in their chapter of history, such as Adam, Abraham, Moses, David, Solomon, Daniel, and hundreds more. The New Testament tells us their deeds were recorded for our profit and that "... these things happened unto them for examples [unto us]" (1 Corinthians 10:11). The examples aren't much good to us unless we take the time to study their lives. On the following pages you will find a suggested character study form which will aid you in such a study. Additional forms are located in the back of the book.

Bible Character Study

Character _____ Main Scripture Passage _____
Date _____

"These things happened unto them as examples unto us."

1. List other passages regarding his life. _____
_____
_____

2. Briefly describe his childhood, parents, family, education._____
_____
_____
_____
_____

3. What character traits do you see in him, both good and bad? _____
_____
_____
_____
_____

4. Describe his main encounter with God. _____
_____
_____
_____
_____

5. Who were his chief companions? Were they a help or a hindrance? _____
_____
_____
_____
_____

6. How did he influence others? _____
_____
_____
_____
_____

Bible Character Study
(continued)

Character _____ Main Scripture Passage _____

Date _____

7. What significant mistakes did he make? _____
_____
_____
_____
_____

8. Did he acknowledge and confess his sins? _____
_____
_____
_____
_____

9. What were his chief contributions in service to God? _____
_____
_____
_____
_____

10. Describe his family life. Was he a good parent? _____
_____
_____
_____
_____

11. How did his children turn out? _____
_____
_____
_____
_____

12. What is the primary lesson of his life that is profitable to you? _____
_____
_____
_____
_____

**Topic
Studies**
One of the ways we know the Bible was authored by God, and not just by the men who wrote it, is its amazing consistency. That is clearly seen in the study of topics in Scripture, for whether you are studying a particular topic in Genesis or Revelation you will always find a unity of thought. In fact, you cannot really know God's mind on a subject until you have examined every reference to that topic in the Bible.

Recently I did a study on the will of God that provides a good example. Christians frequently ask, "How can I find the will of God for my life?" We all have to make many decisions as we go through life, but the tragedy is that very few Christians have taken the time to discover what God has already written about His will. That can be done quite simply: Just look up in a concordance every reference to the will of God in the Bible and write them on a sheet of paper. You will find that some instructions are repeated one or more times. Group them, and then read them over until they fall into a basic pattern. The following is what I discovered:

A. God has a will for your life!
   See Psalm 32:8; Isaiah 58:11; Isaiah 30:21;
   Romans 12:1,2.

B. Examples of God's will:
   Christ—Luke 22:42; John 4:34.

David—Acts 13:22; Acts 13:36.

C. God's will for all people:
1. Repent and be saved:
    1 Timothy 2:4; 2 Peter 3:9; Matthew
    18:14; John 6:40.
2. Be filled with the Spirit:
    Ephesians 5:17-21.
3. Fill your mind with the Word of God:
    Colossians 1:9; Colossians 4:12.
4. Surrender your will and body to Christ:
    Romans 12:1,2.
5. Serve Christ with a willing heart:
    Ephesians 6:6,7.
6. Live a sanctified, morally pure life:
    1 Thessalonians 4:3; 1 Peter 4:2.
7. Give thanks in everything:
    1 Thessalonians 5:18.

D. The reward for doing God's will:
    1 John 2:17.

E. The results of *not* doing God's will:
    Matthew 7:21.

Once you have learned the principles of the
will of God as taught in His Word, you will
find it very easy to know what to do. Igno-
rance destroys God's people and is the cause
of much needless heartache. A simple topic
study helps to avoid such grief, not only on
the subject of the will of God but on a host of
other topics as well. Would you like to know
what God's Word teaches about fear, anger,

sin, adultery, truth, or any other subject? Do a topical study and discover it for yourself.

Prophecy Studies

One very interesting Bible study is prophecy, particularly in this day when many events appear to be fulfillments of Bible prophecies. But keep in mind that the main thrust of the Scriptures is not just prophecy. Instead, they were written about God, the life of Christ, man, salvation, and daily Christian living. Prophecy is dealt with in a number of places throughout the Bible, but in some books it occupies only a chapter or two, while in others it is just one paragraph within a chapter, and in still others it is only a single verse. The following list of Scriptures and their subjects is not intended to be exhaustive, but it will at least give the beginning student a basic knowledge of prophecy:

The Olivet Discourse

Matthew 24, 25

Mark 13

Luke 21 (This is the most important prophetic passage in the Scriptures. It is a basic chronology of events to come given by our Lord.)

The Rapture of Believers

1 Thessalonians 4:13-18

1 Corinthians 15:51-58

The Believer's Judgment

1 Corinthians 3:9-17 (see also 2 Corinthians 5:10; Romans 14:10; 1 Corinthians 4:5)

Russian-Israeli Conflicts	Ezekiel 37-39
The Tribulation Period	2 Thessalonians 2:1-12 (read also Revelation 6-18)
The Glorious Appearing of Christ	Revelation 19:1-21 (see also Revelation 17:14-18; Luke 17:22-37)
The Millennial Kingdom of Christ	Revelation 20:1-10 (see also Isaiah 65:17-25)
The Final Judgment of Lost Souls	Revelation 20:11-15
The New Heaven and Earth	Revelation 21,22

Various descriptions of conditions in the last days just prior to and after the coming of Christ for the church are listed in:

2 Timothy 3:1-4:8—An acceleration of evil
2 Peter 3:1-18—Scoffers and willful man

Few Bible studies will motivate you to greater consecration and service for Christ than prophecy and the second coming of our Lord. "Beloved, now are we the sons of God, and it doth not yet appear what we shall be; but we know that, when he shall appear, we shall be like him, for we shall see him as he is. And every man that hath this hope in him purifieth himself, even as he is pure" (1 John 3:2,3). For a more thorough study of the prophecy passages in the Bible, get a copy of the author's companion book, *How to Study Bible Prophecy for Yourself.*

Christ Studies

Another inspiring topical study is the deity of our Lord. Many verses throughout Scripture give certain insights that together provide us a composite picture of Him. The following list is not complete, but will give you a base on which to start. Your own daily Bible reading will provide many other insights.

Isaiah 52:13–53:12	Christ's First Coming Forecast
Psalm 22:1-31	Christ's Crucifixion Forecast
Luke 1:1-80	Christ's and John the Baptist's Births Forecast
Luke 2:1-52	Christ's Birth and Young Childhood
Matthew 1:1–2:23	More on the Birth of Christ
John 1	Christ the Word
Matthew 3	The Baptism of Jesus

Matthew 4	The Temptation of Christ and Call of the Disciples
John 2	The First Miracle of Christ
John 5	Christ Heals a Crippled Man
John 6:1-14	The Feeding of the Five Thousand
John 6:15-21	Christ Walks on Water
John 9	Christ Heals a Man Born Blind
John 10	Christ the Good Shepherd
John 11	The Raising of Lazarus
John 13	Jesus Washes His Disciples' Feet
John 18	The Mistrial of Jesus
John 19	The Crucifixion
John 20	The Resurrection
John 21	The Post-Resurrection Appearances of Christ
Acts 1	The Ascension of Christ
Revelation 1	The Vision of Christ by John
Revelation 2,3	Christ and the Churches
Philippians 2:1-11	The Self-Emptying of Christ

Jesus' Life and Teachings

Passage_____ Date _____

1. Is the passage about His life or His teaching? _____

2. Give the essential details of the events. _____
_____
_____
_____

3. Who were His friends? _____
_____

4. Who were His enemies? _____
_____

5. Why were they opposed to Him? _____
_____

6. What other passages tell the same story? _____
_____
_____

7. What other details do they include? _____
_____
_____

8. What do you learn about His deity in this passage? _____
_____
_____

9. Everything Jesus did expressed the nature and attitude of God. What did you learn about God in this passage? _____
_____
_____

10. What principles did He teach? _____
_____
_____
_____
_____

11. What can you apply to your life? _____
_____
_____

Jesus' Parables

Name of Parable _____

Passage _____ Date _____

1. What circumstances led up to this teaching, if any? _____
_____
_____
_____

2. Prepare a brief summary of the parable. _____
_____
_____
_____

3. List any additional details given in parallel passages. _____
_____
_____
_____
_____

4. Does He give an interpretation? _____
_____
_____
_____

5. What is the one central truth He is teaching? _____
_____
_____
_____
_____

6. Is there something here for me to apply to my life? If so, how can I do it? ___
_____
_____
_____
_____
_____
_____
_____
_____

Colossians 1:9-23   The Glory and Present Work of Christ

By the time you have done a chapter analysis of each of the above passages, allowing about one week or 1½ hours for each, you will have a thorough knowledge of Christ's life and ministry. The accompanying chart will help you both in the study and in providing a handy review aid in the years to come. Some of our Lord's teachings were in parables, and so we have provided a special chart just for them.

**Psalms
Studies**

The 150 Psalms of the Old Testament provide the Christian with a rich source of practical instruction and information. Some are very short (4-6 verses) and can be analyzed in a few minutes; some are very long (up to 176 verses) and can be broken down into several sections. A majority of the Psalms were written by King David, who, in spite of the terrible sins he committed at one point of his life, was really a dedicated man of God with unique insights. His psalms provide some of the best loved passages in the Bible.

Originally the Psalms were used as the hymn-book of Israel. Many are written in Hebrew parallelism; that is, they say the same thing twice, but in a little different way. The second phrase or verse sometimes just repeats, while at other times it is an amplification of the first phrase. Psalm 102:1,2 is a good example:

Phrase 1—"Hear my prayer, O Lord."

Phrase 2—"Let my cry come unto thee."

Essentially they say the same thing.

Phrase 3—"Hide not thy face from me in the day when I am in trouble."

Phrase 4—"Incline thine ear unto me; in the day when I call, answer me speedily."

Notice that in phrase 4 he adds two things to his petition: He wants God to lean His ear to him and to do so *quickly*. Who can say he has never felt like that?

The word "blessed" occurs frequently throughout the Psalms. Basically this word means "happy." For example, "Blessed is the man that . . . " means "Happy is the man. . . . " You will find that the Psalms contain many practical keys to happiness. It has been my custom for years to prescribe the reading of the Psalms to all who are discouraged or joyless.

Almost all of the Psalms provide a rich Bible study, but the following have been particularly helpful to the author.

Psalm 1 The Introductory Psalm

Psalms Study

Passage_____ Date _____

1. To whom is this Psalm addressed? _____
_____

2. List the blessings and the conditions for receiving them. _____
_____
_____
_____

3. What promises did you find? _____
_____
_____
_____

4. Are there any commands? _____
_____
_____

5. Is there anything that causes you to think particularly of Christ in this Psalm?
_____
_____
_____

6. What is the gist of the Psalm? _____
_____
_____
_____
_____

7. What central thought appeals to you? _____
_____
_____
_____
_____

8. What does this Psalm teach that you can do to be a happier or more blessed
   person? _____
_____
_____
_____
_____

Psalms Study

Passage_____ **Date** _____

1. To whom is this Psalm addressed? _____

_____

2. List the blessings and the conditions for receiving them._____

_____

_____

_____

3. What promises did you find? _____

_____

_____

_____

4. Are there any commands?_____

_____

_____

5. Is there anything that causes you to think particularly of Christ in this Psalm?

_____

_____

_____

6. What is the gist of the Psalm?_____

_____

_____

_____

_____

7. What central thought appeals to you? _____

_____

_____

_____

_____

8. What does this Psalm teach that you can do to be a happier or more blessed
   person? _____

_____

_____

_____

_____

Psalm 8	The Glory of God and His Messiah
Psalm 23	The Great Shepherd Psalm
Psalm 24	Prophecy of Christ
Psalm 27	An Encouragement of Faith
Psalm 34	The Lord Takes Care of His Own
Psalm 37	The Faith-Rest Life
Psalm 51	A Cry for Forgiveness
Psalm 59	A Cry for Help
Psalm 66	Thanksgiving for All of God's Blessings
Psalm 78	God's Dealing with Israel As an Example
Psalm 91	The Best Way to Live
Psalm 103	A Paean of Praise
Psalm 119	God's Description of the Scriptures
Psalm 127	The Blessings of a Family

The previous chart will prove helpful in doing a study of the Psalms.

Proverbs Studies   One of my favorite studies through the years has been the book of Proverbs. It is the best book on principles to live by that has ever been written, and its timeless principles are as important today as they were in the day that God delivered them to Solomon. Like the Psalms, all of the Proverbs are worthy of study, but the following are sure to provide strategic blessing:

Proverbs 1   The Importance of Wisdom

Proverbs 2   Wisdom Saves from Evil

Proverbs 3   Principles for Happy Living

Proverbs 4   A Father's Advice to His Son

Proverbs 6   The Advice of Parents

Proverbs 7   The High Price of Immorality

Proverbs 11   Integrity Living

Proverbs 20   Righteous Living Is a Blessing

Proverbs 22   How to Conduct Your Business Life

Proverbs 24   The Motivation of Righteousness

Proverbs 31   The Virtuous Woman

The following chart will prove helpful in doing a study of Proverbs.

Proverbs Study

Proverb _____ **Date** _____

(The Proverbs were written to make man wise toward God and man.)

1. What is presented as wisdom? _____
_____
_____
_____

2. What negatives are condemned?_____
_____
_____
_____

3. What positives are commended? _____
_____
_____
_____

4. List the timeless principles._____
_____
_____
_____
_____

5. Do you know any other passages that say the same basic thought?_____
_____
_____
_____
_____

6. Is there anything you have been doing that is here condemned?_____
_____
_____
_____

7. Is something taught here that you need to incorporate into your daily life? __
_____
_____
_____

Proverbs Study

Proverb _____ **Date** _____

(The Proverbs were written to make man wise toward God and man.)

1. What is presented as wisdom? _____
_____
_____
_____

2. What negatives are condemned?_____
_____
_____
_____

3. What positives are commended? _____
_____
_____
_____

4. List the timeless principles._____
_____
_____
_____
_____

5. Do you know any other passages that say the same basic thought?_____
_____
_____
_____
_____

6. Is there anything you have been doing that is here condemned?_____
_____
_____
_____

7. Is something taught here that you need to incorporate into your daily life? __
_____
_____
_____

9

How to Study the Bible with Subject Analysis

My mentor in the field of Christian counseling was Dr. Henry Brandt, who held a Ph.D. in the field of psychology. He was the first of his kind to hold the theories of psychology to the test of Scripture. In so doing he developed a ministry for applying biblical principles to the practical problems of life, and in the process he revolutionized the field of Christian counseling. Several of today's most prominent Christian authors in the people-helping field have been influenced by the writings and public teachings of Dr. Brandt.

Henry Brandt was not always a psychologist. His first profession was that of an engineer at the Chrysler plant in Detroit, Michigan, where he became a Christian. Shortly after his conversion he heard his pastor teach, "You don't have a problem in life that cannot be answered by the Word of God." That sounded very encouraging to him, for he was the young father of three children, and every day he was surrounded by men at the plant whose lives were filled with problems.

A few days later one of the engineers at the office began telling Henry about the many problems that he and his wife of 25 years were having. So Brandt replied, "The Bible has the answers to the problems of life." The man then asked what the Bible said about a man being angry in his own home. His wife had said it is wrong, but he felt he just couldn't help it. "After all, a man needs someplace where he can let down his guard and be his real self." Young Brandt didn't know if it was right for a man to be angry or not, so he told him honestly, "I don't know, but I'll go home tonight and study the Bible and see what it says."

That night he got out the only three Christian books he owned: a Bible, a concordance, and a Bible dictionary. His study for the next four hours and his subsequent studies on that subject made him a world authority on anger, and in the process his entire life was changed. A few days after his first study, he stopped his friend at work and told him what his hours of

Bible study revealed: that anger is the most detrimental emotion known to man. It confuses his thinking and inspires violent acts and harmful speech that destroys the closest of friends, particularly married partners, whose anger can turn them into enemies. He also discovered that anger grieves the Holy Spirit, keeping a person from growing spiritually, and in many cases can destroy the body or even bring on premature death. (All these things medical science has now confirmed.)

The next question his friend asked was, "How can I overcome my anger?" Brandt responded, "I don't know, but I'll study the Bible and find out." A few days later he brought in the answer, gleaned from the Bible itself. That first counseling experience for the young engineer changed his marriage. Soon another colleague came to him and said, "Our friend said your Bible has the answers to the problems of life. What does it say about guilt?" The same thing happened; Henry didn't know, but he promised to study the Bible and find out. In the process he began to develop a notebook on what the Bible taught on the basic problems of life. In each case he did the same thing: a subject analysis.

First he looked up all the uses of the word "anger" or "fear" or "lying" or "sin" or whatever problem the men had. Then he would look up the word in a Bible dictionary and write down what the word meant. Then he would look up each verse listed in the concordance and write down the gist of it on a yellow pad. Sometimes he filled six or eight pages with verses. Reading them over carefully, he would pray about the teaching and then write a consensus or an analysis of what God had revealed to him from His Word on that subject.

During the next five years many men were transformed in their personal lives and improved in their interpersonal relationships both at work and at home. Before long Henry was counseling so many people at work that he began to feel guilty about the time he was spending with his troubled fellow employees; after all, Chrysler paid him to be an engineer, not a counselor. Actually, helping the other employees probably was the best thing he did for the company, for once they got their problems worked out they became better employees and accomplished more.

Eventually some of the men began suggesting, "Henry, why don't you go to graduate school and become a psychologist? You seem cut out to counsel people." So he enrolled in night classes at Wayne State University and after two years got his masters degree. Then he enrolled at Cornell University and eventually got his Ph.D. in psychology.

I met Henry Brandt when he was at the peak of his people-helping career, which gave him the authority to challenge the false premises of humanist psychology that had so invaded the church in those days. I can't begin to tell you all the ministers and Christian counselors I knew personally who sounded more like disciples of Freud, Adler, Jung, and other psychologists rather than disciples of Jesus Christ. One highly recommended Christian radio counselor was infamous for saying, "What that person needs is psychological testing and a long series of encounters with a Christian psychologist." Dr. Brandt found that such advice was nonsense. What people needed, according to the Bible, was to face the sin in their life, repent, and confess it to God. Then they should do a Bible study on the subject so the Holy Spirit could give them lasting victory over it. In the process he left a trail of transformed lives all over the country and in many other countries of the world.

Personally, I cannot overstate what Dr. Brandt's teachings did for me in my own personal life, for my marriage, for my wife, for our counseling ministry, and eventually for our writing many people-helping books on depression, anger, temperament, marriage, sexual adjustment, and other topics. I even founded a Family Seminar Ministry that during the past 25 years has taught these biblical principles to over a million people.

In the early years Dr. Brandt did about 50 seminars with me where he often repeated the above story. One night after the first evening's seminars we were talking over coffee, and I asked him how beneficial it was for him to earn his Ph.D. degree. He replied that it had been most helpful in giving him open doors to speak to large audiences or to counsel many needy people. It allowed him to share with them the timeless principles that he had previously learned from the Bible while he was an engineer at Chrysler. That is what made Dr. Brandt different from all other psychologists before him and what enabled him to help untold thousands of people—the timeless principles of the Word of God, firmly entrenched in his mind through Bible study.

The Bible is a literal treasure chest of the "wisdom of God" for everyday living, but most Christians do not know the book sufficiently to provide that wisdom when they need it. I have found that *subject analysis* is the best way to learn the Word of God. It isn't as fast as memorizing, of course, but if you combine this method with memorizing those verses that stand out to you in your subject analysis studies, you will gain a thorough grasp of the Scriptures.

What Subject Analysis Will Do for You

Disciplining yourself to do a thorough analysis of important subjects will make significant demands on your time and mental energy, but the following list of benefits shows that it is well worth it.

1.
It will help you to know what God thinks about major issues.

Doubtless you have heard the expression "I think" or "everyone thinks" or "my father thinks" when in reality what is most important is what *God* thinks. But He is not going to announce His way or will on an issue over a megaphone or on TV. That is not his way of revealing Himself. He has chosen to reveal Himself through *His Word*. Take the subject mentioned above, anger. Many times I have heard people say, "I think there are times when a Christian should get angry!" But does the Bible give them that liberty? That is what is important. Does God hold us accountable to overcome our human tendency to get angry? Only a study of the Bible will tell us. If you do a subject analysis you will find that God held Moses and others accountable for their anger. In fact, it seriously curtailed the longevity of Moses' life and ministry. Obviously, God expected Moses to overcome it.

Even in the one verse that seems to condone anger (Ephesians 4:26), we are commanded not to sin when we get angry. Why? Obviously because that is the most common thing we do when the emotion of anger gets out of control. In my analysis of anger I found 27 verses on the subject, all of which condemn the practice.

The point is that nothing opens your mind better to the wisdom of God than analyzing what the Bible teaches on a subject.

**2.
It will help
you to know
God in a
personal way.**

One of the major purposes of Bible study is to know God, for as we have seen, He reveals Himself to us through His Word. Most Christians, I fear, only learn about God from their pastor's sermons or through special speakers, Christian books, and other literature. These all have a place in our growth, but nothing will help us to know God personally like studying His Word for ourselves. Just as we get to know other people through conversations or correspondence with them, so we get to know God through the study of His Word, which may be likened to having a personal letter from Him.

**3.
It will help
you to love
God.**

To know God is to love Him. But you cannot love anyone you do not know. Very honestly, for many years of my Christian life I did not love God. I believed in Him, I feared Him and respected Him, but I did not love Him. The reason was that I had accepted a false characterization of God. I had not been taught that He was a "merciful God," as the prophet Jonah described Him, or that He was a "loving God," as illustrated by giving His Son for our salvation. I had only been taught that He was the autocratic Judge of the universe. Not until I began doing a subject analysis about God, His holiness, His love for mankind (including me), his "gift of eternal life," and the many other things that more properly describe Him did I come to really love Him and accept Him as my Father in heaven, as Jesus taught.

4. It will give you a complete grasp of all that God wants you to know about a given subject.

We have already seen that the Bible is not a single book; it is a library of 66 books. If we study only one subject, such as atonement, rewards, eternity, or the second coming, from one book or one chapter, we will learn only that one perspective of the subject. It will be correct, but to understand the *entire* subject as God wants us to, we should learn *all* that He has written on that subject.

For example, take the subject of free will or divine sovereignty, a subject on which many Christians disagree. If you study only certain verses that emphasize one side of the subject over the other, you will come to an inadequate conclusion. Everyone who believes the Bible recognizes that God is the Almighty Sovereign of the universe who "chooses" or "elects" or "calls" those who should be saved.

Only by studying all the verses on those subjects, however, do you understand that God's selection is based on His foreknowledge of what choice man will make. Nothing man does comes as a surprise to God. He knows all things, even "the end from the beginning." He knew before the foundations of the world who would and who would not accept Him by faith.

Subject analysis will give you a complete understanding of the revealed mind of God on a given subject. Many Christians settle for an inadequate view of God and a casual relationship with Him because they have never learned what He has taught us about Himself from His Word.

How to Do a Subject Analysis

It would be hard to improve on the above procedure followed by Dr. Brandt. It made him into one of the greatest biblical counselors of our day. It will help you to become "a workman who does not need to be ashamed, rightly dividing the word of truth" (2 Timothy 2:15 NKJV), and a "man of God [who] may be complete, thoroughly equipped for every good work" (2 Timothy 3:17 NKJV). In my opinion, nothing will complete your understanding of biblical truth like your own personal subject analysis, which is really easy enough to be done by anyone. Follow these simple steps:

1. Look the subject up in a good concordance—*Young's Analytical Concordance* or one that is less exhaustive, *Cruden's Concordance*.

2. Write down on a notepad each new concept on that subject. Understand that many teachings or concepts are repeated in Scripture to different people or by different writers. Whenever God says anything, that reveals His mind on the matter.

3. Look up all references to that subject, particularly those in the New Testament and in two of the Wisdom books of the Old Testament.

God has revealed to us the things necessary to the Christian life in the New Testament. An example is the Ten Commandments. The only commandment not mentioned in the New Testament is "Remember the Sabbath to keep it holy." Why was it omitted? Because that is the only commandment He changed from the Old Testament. That command was given before Christ was crucified and rose again on the first day of the week. As far back as we have records in the early life of the church, the believers met on Sunday as a testimony to the Savior's resurrection. The reason I also include the books of Psalms and Proverbs is because they were given by God through the wisest man who ever lived or ever would live, Solomon, and the man who taught him most of his wisdom, King David. Both deal in practical everyday principles for living the best kind of life.

4. Study your notations carefully. Read them over several times until the central teachings begin to come clear. Educators say that repetition is an aid to learning.

5. Begin making a list of the concepts or basic principles that God is teaching on that subject. This should be reduced to one or at most two pages.

6. Try to reduce your analysis of the subject to one paragraph (half a page at most).

7. Go to a good Bible dictionary and examine the definition of that same subject. I recommend the *Holman Bible Dictionary*, available in Christian bookstores. If your analysis is seriously different from theirs, then you should go back over your first page of documentation and your analysis to see if you missed something in your own study. If so, write in a paragraph

describing where you agree and another where you disagree. If you agree with the dictionaries, praise the Lord and go on to the next subject.

Most subjects can be carefully analyzed in 30 to 60 minutes a week. Some complex subjects may take two or three hours. If you keep at it consistently, you can compile a notebook of 30 or more subject analyses a year. Within one month you will find this to be one of the most exciting methods of Bible study you have ever tried.

Tools for Bible Study

A craftsman will always have excellent tools. No workman will become a craftsman unless he has the right ones. The same is true of the Bible student. His tools are the Bible and good books about the Bible.

Most young Bible students tend to make one of two mistakes when it comes to Bible study aids. They either reject them altogether and study only the Bible, or they read so many books about the Bible that they rarely read the Bible itself. Both approaches are wrong.

So far we have given many practical suggestions that will help the earnest young convert gain a good working knowledge of the Word of God in just three years. Now it is time to consider some invaluable tools or aids to Bible study.

Ten Essential Books

It is only natural that as a minister and author I am a lover of books. From the days when I devoured 19 Zane Grey novels for a high school English literature class until the present, I have been an avid reader. (I'm a great believer that you are what you read.) Consequently I have several thousand dollars' worth of books in my study and home library.

But *it isn't necessary* that you buy that many! In fact, I have developed a list of only ten books that I consider essential for your library. You will find in these books all you basically need for your first three years of Bible studies. The following ten books, with a description of each, are listed in order of their importance. In some cases I include optional selections in the same category. You should not get two books in one category until you have one in all ten. A good way to painlessly collect these books is to put them on your birthday or Christmas list.

1.
A Good
Bible

The first and foremost requirement for becoming a Bible student is a good Bible. You are probably well aware of the fact that there are all kinds of Bibles on the market, from translations and paraphrases to mistranslations. How are you to know what is best? If you are not a Greek or Hebrew scholar, you will have to take the word of those who are. Among those scholars of my acquaintance, the preferences are one of the following three Bibles.

The New Scofield Reference Bible

For over 50 years the Scofield Reference Bible, first produced in 1909 by lawyer-Bible teacher C.I. Scofield, was the most popular Bible of choice by sincere students attending Bible-believing fundamental churches and Bible conferences. Its timely and practical footnotes and helps, along with the paragraph headings, made Bible reading and study very interesting. It was updated in 1967 by a committee of Bible scholars that eliminated some of the old archaic words, but it lags behind the many easier-to-understand modern translations of today. Its greatest attraction is the same-page footnotes with helps and insights given to the original meanings that are usually quite dependable.

The New King James Version

The New King James Version of the Bible (NKJV), published in 1982, is a significant improvement over the King James Version (KJV), which for four centuries was the most loved and used English version in use. Recognizing that over 400 words had changed their meanings since the KJV was first produced in 1611, a group of reliable scholars were brought together to produce an accurate update of that much-loved translation, limiting change to only what was necessary to promote accuracy and clarity.

Consequently, the NKJV retains much of the dignity and beauty of the older version (which goes back to William Tyndale, of the fourteenth century) while making it easier for people today to understand. This NKJV version was produced by more Greek and Hebrew scholars and tested by more popular Bible teachers than any Bible translation since the original KJV. Some scholars say it is the most reliable version in print today.

The New International Version

The New International Version (NIV) was first published in its entirety in 1978 and has already become the most popular Bible of our times, due no doubt to its modern easy-to-understand reading style. It is almost as easy to read as the popular Living Bible, but it more accurately adheres to the original languages, though it does have its scholarly critics. If any modern Bible replaces the old King James Version as the most-read text in worship services, it will probably be the NIV. It is enormously popular among the younger generation.

Many new study Bibles have appeared during the past decade that have sparked renewed interest in Bible study. One of the favorites is the Inductive Study Bible, designed by Kay Arthur of Precept Ministries and published by

Harvest House. It provides a balance of background study material for the new student, yet allows the reader to determine for himself the message that God has for him or her. The Life Recovery Bible is a favorite among prisoners and other Bible students who are willing to be diligent in regularly reading and studying the Word of God. The Thompson Chain-Reference Bible has much to commend it, as does the Open Bible, which now can be purchased in the New King James Version as well as the King James.

Personally, I prefer the NKJV for my own Bible study and the NIV for long-term, enjoyable reading. The new Christian, however, would be advised to select one version and stick to it until he becomes familiar with it before bouncing back and forth among versions. The Bible was actually written by man, but in reality they were inspired by God the Holy Spirit; therefore when you read the Scriptures, listen for the voice of God, your heavenly Father. Of the several reliable versions mentioned here (including the New American Standard Version, if that is your preference), whichever aids you to recognize His message best, use that one. Even more important than which version you use is that you use it on a near-daily basis.

2. Halley's Bible Handbook

One of the most helpful books ever written on the whole Bible for young Christians is *Halley's Bible Handbook*. Over 3 million copies in print tells the story of its popularity. It is recommended by more ministers, Bible teachers, and Christian workers than any other book of its kind. Its 860 pages provide the reader with more biblical information than any other book its size. Although it is not a complete commentary, it does tell the reader something about every book in the Bible. It also gives a great deal of fascinating information about archeological findings that confirm biblical accuracy, important information about the silent years between the Testaments, and much additional helpful material.

This book was not intended for scholars but is a very practical and readable book designed to inspire laypeople to read and enjoy their Bible. Popularly priced, it is the best Bible study help for the price available today.

3. A Bible Concordance

An invaluable help in studying the Bible is a concordance containing all the verses in the Scripture on a given subject. It provides the simplest method of determining what the full teaching of God is on that particular theme. As we saw in the previous chapter, a concordance is indispensable for subject studies. We noted that there is much confusion today among counselors on the subject of anger. Some justify it, others suggest that it should be channeled into energy, some are afraid of repressing it, etc. Much of this confusion is eliminated when we study the more than 200 verses on anger in the Scripture. We find that anger is a sin that grieves the Holy Spirit, causes murder, is contagious, and should not dominate a Spirit-controlled Christian's life. Such a study of anger is really quite simple, for all the references in the Bible on that subject are found on one page in a concordance.

The best concordance on the market, in this writer's opinion, is *Strong's Exhaustive Concordance*, by James Strong. It is large and a little cumbersome, but it contains the most complete listing of subjects and references available. In addition to including all the words in the Bible, it contains both a Hebrew and a Greek dictionary with a handy method of looking up the original words. The proper pronunciation of each word in its original language is given along with the best meaning. This feature enables even those that are not language scholars to go to the root word and check its accuracy. This is particularly important in a day when we have so many translations to choose from, many of which contradict each other. How is the layman supposed to know which is right? *Strong's Exhaustive Concordance* provides the answer.

Another possibility that has been used by millions of Bible students for the past seven decades is *Cruden's Complete Concordance*. Much smaller than *Strong's Concordance* (and also somewhat lighter), it is easier to use but lacks some of the helps of *Strong's*. You may find it useful to have both, since *Cruden's* helps you to quickly locate those verses you can vaguely remember but can't find, while *Strong's* helps you do a thorough study of words or subjects.

Those who use the New International Version would be advised to get *The NIV Complete Concordance* so that the words of the newer translations match those in the concordance. Otherwise you will have difficulty finding some subjects you will need to locate. Don't be surprised if you wear out at least one concordance in your lifetime.

4.
A Bible
Dictionary

Another vital tool for Bible study is a good Bible dictionary. Frequently you will find subjects, words, places, or doctrines that need to be described fully. Where is a young convert to look for an accurate meaning? The same place he would look for anything—a dictionary or encyclopedia, except that those found in the average public library do not always include all Bible subjects. In addition, they are often written from a hostile or anti-Christian point of view. A Bible dictionary contains a thorough listing of all Bible subjects and was compiled or authored by someone specifically trained in the Bible and its customs, places, and teachings.

In the first edition of this book I recommended the 1192-page *Unger's Bible Dictionary*, by Dr. Merrill F. Unger, published by Moody Press. I used it enjoyably for many years and on occasions still do. But I have found the 1500-page *Holman Bible Dictionary*, published in 1991, to be superior in several respects. It is easier to read, has over 600 color photographs, and is truly reader-friendly. It covers almost every subject that most Bible students need to investigate and presents the material in a historically and archeologically accurate manner with the latest evidence supporting and explaining biblical truth.

5.
A One-Volume Bible Commentary

Because of the antiquity of the Bible, its occasionally heavy theological subjects, and the fact that it was written in a language and to a people quite different from our own, it is very helpful to have a trustworthy Bible commentary to turn to when a passage does not seem too clear. There are so many such commentaries available that it is difficult to select the best one because personal opinion and usage enter into one's evaluation. But it does seem to me that a young Bible student could easily get bogged down in an exhaustive commentary, plus the fact that multivolumed commentaries are quite expensive. For that reason I recommend a single-volume commentary, for ease of use and low expense.

Matthew Henry's Commentary, published by Zondervan Publishing House, has been a favorite of many Bible students for many years. Somewhat wordy in its original five-volume set, it has been edited down to one thick 2000-page volume that contains the heart of Henry's comments on the Scriptures. Largely devotional in nature, it is popular among ministers and Bible students. Someone has said that Charles H. Spurgeon, one of the greatest preachers who ever lived, used it continuously. Although it has not helped me to preach like Spurgeon, I have used it for at least 25 years.

A more contemporary commentary has been published by Moody Press entitled *The Wycliffe Bible Commentary*. This 1500-page work provides scholarly comments and insights on every book in the Bible, and deals with almost every passage as it appears. Still another single-volume commentary that is worth studying is the 1985 release of

Gaebelein's Concise Commentary on the Whole Bible, published by Loizeaux Brothers. It is a condensed version of the author's popular four-volume set that has blessed Bible students for half a century. It has a warmth of personal application that is often lacking in other commentaries which makes it a must for both Bible students and teachers.

**6.
The Bible
Has the
Answer**

There are approximately 150 basic questions that come to people's minds as they study the Bible. Dr. Henry M. Morris, one of the world's finest scholars and Bible students, has compiled these questions, and together with his friend, Dr. Martin Clark, give some clear and helpful Bible answers to them in *The Bible Has the Answer.* For example, "How do you know the Bible is true?" "How do you know God exists?" "How can one God be three Persons?" "Was Jesus a revolutionary?" "Has modern science discredited the Bible?" "Was Jonah really swallowed by a whale?" and about 144 others. The authors have selected some of life's most difficult questions and have dealt with them biblically and practically. The publisher is Master Books, and it is available through the Institute for Creation Research, P.O. Box 2667, El Cajon, CA 92021. You will find much help in this book.

7.
Many
Infallible
Proofs

Although God commands man to accept Him by faith, He does not expect man to accept Him by *blind* faith. What is the difference? The Bible and the human mind. Man's mind will never come to faith on its own, but when guided by the revelation of God and the Bible, man can logically believe in God. Dr. Henry M. Morris again has produced a superb book setting out clearly the logical reasons for accepting such subjects as "the virgin birth," "the nature of God," "the resurrection of Christ," "the inspiration of the Bible," "fulfillments of prophecy," "alleged contradictions in Scripture," "scientific fallacies of evolution," and many others. A new and updated version of this book with the latest scientific discoveries that support the Bible, containing more evidences for the Christian faith, was published in 1996 by Master Books. It is available in most Christian bookstores or from the Institute for Creation Research, P.O. Box 2667, El Cajon, CA 92021. This excellent volume should be read carefully by every Christian who would know the Scriptures and why he believes them.

8.
A Harmony
of the
Gospels

The beginning Bible student may find the events in the life of Christ as presented in one Gospel somewhat confusing when compared with that of another. Because each Gospel had a different author and was written to a different group of people or had a slightly different perspective, some of the events may at first appear to be contradictory. False teachers have seized on such seeming variations in the account to suggest that the Bible is not reliable. In truth, there are no contradictions in the Bible, but many people who are unlearned in the Scriptures have experienced a spiritual setback at thinking there might be.

Johnston M. Cheney had such an experience. As a young man, his faith was so shaken that he even questioned his salvation for a time. Fortunately, he didn't stop studying the Word of God, and gradually his faith and confidence in God's Word returned as he saw the answers to his questions emerge one by one as he scrutinized the passages in question. For 20 years he pored over the four Gospels until he almost had them memorized. When he had every seeming inconsistency adequately explained, he decided to write a careful harmony of the Gospels to show how each event fits into the totality of our Lord's life. His excellent book, *The Life of Christ in Stereo*, published by Western Baptist Seminary Press, will help all who have questions in harmonizing the events of Scripture.

9. Bible Doctrine

The basic teachings of the Bible are often called "doctrines," meaning the special teachings that are unique to the Scriptures. Since these doctrines are not taught consecutively (because the Bible was written historically, and thus the doctrinal teachings occur all through the Scriptures), all the passages bearing on a given subject have to be studied carefully in order to come to a complete understanding of the teaching. Such study requires years of training and research time, which the Christian layman seldom has available.

Fortunately, many great Bible scholars have written books explaining the most basic doctrinal concepts. Those which every student should know include the nature of God, the life and work of Christ, the Holy Spirit, the Bible, the nature of man, the future destiny of Christians, and a host of other subjects. My favorite book of Bible doctrines is *What the Bible Teaches,* by R. A. Torrey, published by Fleming H. Revell Company. Another good book on this subject is *Great Doctrines of the Bible,* by Dr. William Evans, published by Moody Press. Victor Books has also published another excellent source for Bible doctrine, *Basic Theology*, subtitled, *A Popular Systematic Guide to Understanding Biblical Truth,* by Dr. Charles C. Ryrie, the author of the excellent Ryrie Study Bible.

**10.
The Super-
naturalness
of Christ**

Jesus Christ is the heart of the Bible and the center of the Christian faith. If indeed He is the supernatural Son of God, we can accept everything He said as "gospel truth." The beginning student of Scripture would be wise not only to "believe in Jesus Christ unto salvation" but also to know the good logical reasons for his belief.

Every Christian is confronted with questions or claims by skeptics that he cannot answer immediately, or else the circumstances of life cause him serious doubts. Nothing calms those fears and inspires faith like studying the overwhelming evidence for the fact that Jesus Christ was indeed who He claimed to be— God in human flesh. This is so important that in the first edition of this book I recommended the classic *The Supernaturalness of Christ,* by one of the greatest Christian scholars of the twentieth century (and also one of my earliest professors), Dr. Wilbur Smith.

Unfortunately, that book is now out of print, which together with the overpublicized attacks on the deity of Christ and the credibility of the Bible by the Jesus Seminar skeptics inspired me to write my latest book, *Jesus: Who Is He?* (1997). It is an easy-to-read, logical presentation of the awesome evidence for Christ's deity. It is intended to inspire faith and dedication in

the heart of all believers and to confront unbe-
lievers with all the evidence they need to make
their commitment to Christ. Many of the best
concepts of Dr. Smith's book were used and
expanded in mine.

Most of the books on the above list are reference books that you will use many times in
life. This last one is must reading for every
young Christian. It will give you an answer to
those who ask for a reason for the confidence
you have in the Christian faith. Before your
three-year study of the Word is concluded,
you should read this book. I am convinced
that no Christian ever loses his faith for lack
of evidence. It has been lack of *exposure* to
that evidence that causes a loss of faith. I
doubt that anyone can read *Jesus: Who Is He?*
with an open mind and not be convinced that
God has given us overwhelming evidence
upon which to build our belief in Christ's
deity, which is the cornerstone of our faith.

No group of ministers will agree on the ten
most important books for the beginning Bible
student, but these have proven extremely
helpful to me through the years. I have recommended them to many others and am con-
fident you will find them profitable—if you
use them.

11

Hermeneutics

Hermeneutics is a careful method of Bible study that ensures that the message God intended to communicate is accurately understood by man. The Bible is not a simple book, but it is a divine communication with humanity which uses human authors to do the communicating. The reason a scientific method of study like hermeneutics is necessary is seen in the diagram on page 158.

An infinite God who is a spirit knows everything about everything. The difficulty in communicating with man, His creature, is that man has only limited amount of intuitive knowledge and must use his eyes and ears, for that is the way man learns most things. The problem is further complicated because man speaks various languages; therefore God chose to express His infinite concepts in one basic

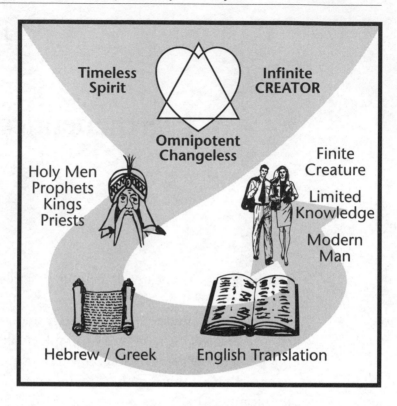

Timeless
Spirit

Infinite
CREATOR

Omnipotent
Changeless

Holy Men
Prophets
Kings
Priests

Finite
Creature

Limited
Knowledge

Modern
Man

Hebrew / Greek   English Translation

language and have it translated into the various other languages of mankind.

Again, the communication process is complicated in that words, idioms, and customs have changed during the over 3500 years since God first began revealing His mind and will to man in a written record. Therefore, there must be some accurate system devised to guarantee that what God said and meant so long ago is what present translations say and mean to modern man. That accurate system is known as hermeneutics. It is a logical, scholarly, and trustworthy attempt to accurately assure that modern man understands the message that God originally set out to communicate to him. The following hermeneutic rules guide the careful students of all generations to "rightly divide the Word of Truth."

Rules of Hermeneutics

1.
Take
the Bible
literally

Much harm has been done by trying to "spiritualize" the Bible instead of taking it literally. When a person writes you a letter you do not normally "spiritualize" its meaning, but you take it literally to heart. The same is true of the Bible. There are, however, some few passages in the Scriptures that should be taken nonliterally or "spiritually". The question is, "How is the student to know which passages should be taken literally and which ones spiritually?" The best answer I know is the Golden Rule of Interpretation, designed by the late Bible scholar Dr. David L. Cooper:

> When the plain sense of Scripture makes common sense, seek no other sense, but take every word at its primary literal meaning unless the facts of the immediate context clearly indicate otherwise.

You will rarely go wrong in Bible study if you first try to interpret a passage literally. For example, when the Bible says, "Fire and brimstone fell out of heaven," it literally means that fire and brimstone came down on the earth. When, however, the Bible says that the moon turned to blood or the Nile River turned to blood, as it did in the days of Moses, it does not mean that it literally turned to blood, but that it turned to a bloodlike color. However, even in the case of the Nile River, this resulted in the death of fish. A good rule to follow is try to interpret each passage literally. If this is obviously not the case, then as a last resort try to find the spiritual or symbolical truth it is communicating.

**2.
Keep it
in context**

It is always good to use Scripture verses to prove a teaching or principle, but it is important not to lift a verse out of its context; otherwise, as we have previously seen, instead of it being a prooftext, it becomes a pretext.

**3.
Watch for
idioms**

Every language has its idioms. In fact, idioms are one of the most complex parts of language study. For example, have you ever thought about the difficulty encountered by foreigners in learning English when they come upon such common idioms as "saved by the skin of your teeth"? One of the things that complicates the use of idioms is that they change their meaning from one generation to another.

For example, my teenage children were quite put out with me one time when I asked their group, "How are you making out?" only to find that the term "making out" had changed its meaning since I was their age. Usually a good Bible commentary will point out the idiomatic use of language and explain the meaning in the day in which it was written.

4.
Be alert to the figurative use of language

When language is not used literally, the author will often resort to figures of speech. We are accustomed to that in English. For example, during a radio broadcast of a World Series baseball game the announcer said the base runner was "hugging" third base. Obviously, he did not mean the man picked up the base and hugged it. Later he announced that the batter hit a foul ball that "hugged" third base. He meant it was close, but in that instance it was not a fair ball. But when the pitcher struck out the last batter to win the World Series, he described how the catcher rushed out to the mound and "hugged" the pitcher. Each use of the verb "hug" meant something different, and only one use meant a literal, physical hug. The context is the key. So it is in Bible study: The *context* will tell you when to take a word literally and when to find a figurative meaning.

You are probably familiar with the five most common figures of speech: metaphor, simile, analogy, hyperbole, and personification. We shall examine each of these briefly.

Metaphor   A metaphor compares two things by identifying one with the other. Usually one of the metaphors is easily recognized and is used to clarify the other that is not so easily understood. It is the way we communicate from the known to the unknown. For example, Matthew 5:13 states, "Ye are the salt of the earth," meaning that just as salt is a flavoring influence in food, so Christians should be a flavoring influence morally in their society.

It is the use of metaphors that has given rise to spiritualizing Scripture, because most metaphors are symbols. The most important metaphor in all of Scripture is found in Luke 22:19,20, where Jesus took bread and said, "This is my body, which is given for you." The bread was bread; it was not Christ's literal body. Obviously, it was a *symbol* of His physical body. The same is said of the cup, when He said, "This cup is the new covenant in my blood." We do not drink the blood of Christ when we partake of the grape juice; instead, we drink grape juice, which *symbolizes* His blood. To the careful reader trying to literalize Scripture, the use of metaphors is not really a problem because they are usually quite obvious.

Simile   A simile compares two things, and usually the words "like" or "so" or "as" are used to introduce them. For example, our Lord said in Matthew 10:16, "Behold, I send you forth as sheep in the midst of wolves." The obvious simile is in comparing Christians to sheep and false teachers to wolves. This is a basic simile that is used in many places in Scripture. Again, it is usually not difficult to recognize similes.

Analogy   An analogy is a comparison of two things wherein one explains the other. Usually an analogy is used as a type of reasoning. For example, in 1 Corinthians 1:18 Paul said, "For the preaching of the cross is to them that perish foolishness, but unto us which are saved it is the power of God."

Hyperbole   A hyperbole is a deliberate attempt to exaggerate for the purpose of attracting attention. For example, in Matthew 7:3 our Lord said, "And why beholdest the mote that is in thy brother's eye but considerest not the beam that is in thine own eye?" Obviously no man could have a literal beam in his eye, but this hyperbole calls attention through exaggeration to the tragic result of criticism.

Personification   This word essentially means ascribing human characteristics to God. The Bible teaches that God is a spirit and consequently does not have a body. But it is impossible for man to understand a spirit. Therefore it was essential for God to use human-body characteristics to describe Himself, and thus we find the Lord's "ear" or the Lord's "voice" or the Lord's "hand." God hears us and He speaks to man and He sustains man, but He does not have literal eyes or hands or ears as we do. But in His own divine way He accomplishes the same result. Therefore He uses the finite characteristics of man, which man can easily understand, to describe His own infinite characteristics, which otherwise man could not understand. It is wrong to infer, as some have, that God has *literal* ears and hands like man.

5.
Treat parables differently

A parable is an earthly story with a heavenly meaning. The best way to see the need for parabolic teaching is to envision yourself as a missionary in a remote area where the people have never seen electricity, refrigeration, or any modern inventions. How would you describe to such people the appliances in your kitchen? You would have to painstakingly use something within their frame of reference to use as a picture or parable to convey your meaning. The same is true in communicating heavenly or divine truth. Jesus Christ was a master at using parables. Often these parables are introduced by the statement "The kingdom of heaven is like . . ." or "A certain man went into a far country. . . ."

When it comes to interpreting parables, many people overwork them; that is, they try to make every single detail mean something special. But in so doing they often destroy the basic meaning. A parable is an *illustration;* when you give an illustration of something you are trying to communicate, it has *one central truth.* Almost every illustration can be distorted and twisted way out of proportion by trying to apply every segment of it to something specific. For that reason you should be content to find the one central meaning of a parable and accept it.

These five simple rules are not all the rules of hermeneutics, but they are the ones that you should familiarize yourself with because they are the ones you are most likely to confront. You will find that their literal application to Bible study will produce an accurate interpretation of God's message to mankind.

12

Accelerating the Learning Process

Blessed is the man who walketh not in the counsel of the ungodly, nor standeth in the way of sinners, nor sitteth in the seat of the scornful. But his delight is in the law of the Lord, and in his law doth he meditate day and night. And he shall be like a tree planted by the rivers of water, that bringeth forth its fruit in its season; its leaf also shall not wither, and whatsoever he doeth shall prosper (Psalm 1:1-3).

Wherewithal shall a young man cleanse his way? By taking heed thereto according to thy word (Psalm 119:9).

Thy word have I hid in mine heart, that I might not sin against thee (Psalm 119:11).

Scientists tell us there are 12 billion brain cells in the average human mind, but most people only use 10 percent of their brain's potential. Before the use of notepads and handy writing materials, people developed the habit of remembering much of what they heard; it was the only way they had of recalling things from the past which they needed.

In recent years there has been a revival of this lost art of memorizing, and I have observed that those who use it to learn Scripture grow rapidly in their spiritual lives. Dawson Trotman, founder of the Navigators, probably inspired more people to memorize the Word of God than anyone in the twentieth century. He said, "Nothing pays greater dividends for the time invested than writing God's Word on the tablets of the heart." I have seen many individuals take spiritual giant steps as soon as they started memorizing Scripture.

You Can Memorize!

When it comes to memorizing, most people confess to a "mental block." But only in rare instances is that really true. Most of the time the problem is an *ambition* block. If I were to ask for your address or phone number, you would have no trouble recalling it. Anyone who can do that can memorize Bible verses. Very honestly, memorization involves hard work, but it pays greater dividends to your spiritual life than any other known method of Bible study.

What Memorizing Scripture Will Do for You

1.
It gives you victory over sin

"Thy word have I hid in my heart, that I might not sin against thee" (Psalm 119:11). Nothing puts the brakes on a temptation to sin like the Word of God tucked away in the mind. Many a defeated, sin-enslaved Christian has turned into a spiritual giant by learning the Word of God. Most of the sins that "so easily beset us" don't really overpower us, but just ease us over the line between temptation and obedience. The red light of the Word of God flashing in our mind when temptation rears its ugly head is often enough to stop us in our tracks. Each time you heed the Word and reject the inclination to sin, you strengthen your spiritual life and make it easier to refuse sin the next time. Victory over sin is a gradual process, and memorizing the Word speeds up that process.

2.
It helps you overcome worry

Worry, anxiety, and fear are as natural to a human being as building dams are to beavers. That's why the Word of God has so much to say about "fear not," "let not your heart be troubled," and "take no anxious thought for tomorrow." But such injunctions are of little value if you don't have them cemented in your mind when you need them.

Many times as a college president, pastor, founder of Family Life Seminars, and founder of a kindergarten-through-high-school Christian school system, I have been tempted to panic in the face of budgets totaling over 10 million dollars annually. When I looked at the economy and the many family heads who depended on these ministries for their livelihood, I was tempted to panic, particularly in times of recession or inflation. On such occasions my treasure-house of memorized Scripture brought welcome relief by flooding my mind with the principles of God. Mentally saying, "What in the world are we going to do?" did nothing for me. But rehearsing in my mind the promise "My God shall supply *all* your need according to His riches in glory by Christ Jesus" certainly did.

3.
It gives you confidence in sharing your faith

Once you become a Christian you have a natural desire to see others come to Christ. But cold, naked fear is the most common deterrent to witnessing there is. The greatest fear most Christians have is that they either don't know what to say or will say the wrong thing. That can almost never happen if you have made a habit of memorizing key verses. You don't have to be a superextrovert or a great debater to be a good witness for Christ. But you must know some of the key witnessing verses to be effective.

The first time I really saw the power of the Word in the mind of a Christian was in hearing the testimony of a former submarine sailor named Rosenberger. This convert from Judaism told how he rejected everything supernatural and blatantly ridiculed Christians. A brand-new convert was assigned a bunk next to his and Rosenberger caught him memorizing his "three verses a week," as taught by his Navigator buddies just before his ship sailed for the Pacific. The lad didn't know any Christian arguments with which to answer Rosenberger's taunts and sarcastic barbs; all he knew was Bible verses, so each time he answered with "the Bible says . . ." and quoted a verse. Ten months of that was all Rosenberger could stand before bowing to the forgiving grace of God. The heavenly Father says of His Word, "My word...shall not return unto me void, but it shall accomplish that which I please..." (Isaiah 55:11). He makes no such promises for *our* words.

A Christian going out to witness without arming himself with the Word of God is like a soldier going into battle without a weapon.

**4.
It speeds up
the trans-
forming
process**

All Christians are challenged to be "trans-formed"—that is, to walk like "new creatures" (2 Corinthians 5:17). This doesn't happen overnight; it is the result of a long process of growth. Memorizing Scripture, however, will speed up the process remarkably because the secret to transformation is "renewing your mind" (Romans 12:2) through the Word of God. The more Scripture you learn and incorporate into your life, the faster you will conform your life to the wisdom of God as the Bible teaches.

This renewing of the mind by memorizing the Word is particularly effective in changing your thought life. Most men have to fight mentally to keep themselves from lustful thoughts and evil imaginations. Memorizing Scripture gives them something positive to think about rather than just guarding against harmful thoughts. This same technique has proven helpful to those who have to guard their thoughts against envy, resentment, revenge, or other thought patterns that are contrary to God's will for our minds.

**5.
It helps
you avoid
humanistic
influences**

The secularist philosophy dominates education, media, and the entertainment industry today. One of the reasons so many Christians suffer a lapse of faith in college is because they have so little "wisdom of God" safeguarding their minds through Scripture memory. Thus they become vulnerable to "the wisdom of this world" when their professors bombard their minds with secular humanism.

I found in graduate school that the false theories of humanistic psychology that permeated my counseling training violated the many scriptural principles I had already learned by memorizing Scripture. Consequently, I was able to reject them before they took root and influenced my thinking. "Man's wisdom," as the apostle Paul calls it (See 1 Corinthians chapters 1-3), is very subtle and appeals to the human mind. The only safeguard is "the wisdom of God" as it is revealed in Scripture. And the best way to learn that wisdom is to memorize it.

6.
It helps you discover God's will

Sometimes you have to make instant decisions in life; there is no time to run to your Bible or notebook studies. With a backlog of Scriptures stored in the cells of your brain, you will find it much easier to make the right decisions.

7.
It helps you in your other Bible studies

The best commentary on the Bible is the Bible itself. The more basic verses you have in your mind the easier it is for you to understand Scripture in the light of other Scripture. Young Christians often spend a lot of time reading commentaries about the Bible. But after you learn Scripture you will find that commentaries will take less of your time and may be used only when confronting a difficult passage or in preparation for a public message.

8.
It outfits you
for unlimited
service to
God

Through the years I have noticed that many college graduates end up in a profession quite unrelated to either their major or minor course of study. The reason for this is that colleges, particularly Christian colleges, provide a broad base from which to launch a professional career. The door of opportunity usually opens to a person who is successfully occupied. The education gives him the background to be professionally flexible. Memorizing Scripture does the same for a Christian. There is almost no limit to the potential of the child of God who has a good mental grasp on the Bible.

How to Effectively Memorize Scripture

The best way I know of for memorizing the Word is to use Scripture memory cards. Some people use 3 x 5 cards and some use the smaller calling cards, but the important thing is that you carry your current memory cards with you wherever you go. That way you can review your verses during handy moments throughout the day—waiting in the dentist's office, at the bus stop, as you drive to work, or whenever you have a spare moment to "redeem the time." The following suggestions will help simplify your memorization.

1. Write the verse on cards

Copying the verse right from Scripture onto a card in your own handwriting is helpful in starting the memorizing process. Having them typed up looks better, but it doesn't do as much for your mind initially.

2. Learn the verse by topics

Just learning verses and their references can be rather confusing unless you take a few seconds longer to learn a subject or topic for each verse. Rather than learn 50 random verses, it is far more effective to learn one verse for 50 different subjects. The reason for this is that the mind functions by subjects. When you want a verse on prayer or some other subject, it is simple to think of one if you assigned that topic to the verse when you learned it. The examples below illustrate the point.

Prayer

Hitherto have ye asked nothing in my name; ask and ye shall receive, that your joy may be full (John 16:24).

Scripture Memory Commanded

This book of the law shall not depart out of thy mouth, but thou shalt meditate therein day and night, that thou mayest observe to do according to all that is written therein; for then thou shalt make thy way prosperous, and then thou shalt have good success (Joshua 1:8).

Several experts in this field suggest that it is best to learn three verses for each basic Bible subject before going to the next topic. There are two reasons for this. First, it is easier to remember verses in groups of three if you originally learned them this way than it is to learn one verse each for 50 subjects. Second, if you are a young Christian, some subjects are more important for you to memorize at first than others. At the end of this chapter is a list of three verses for 50 different subjects that you should learn in your program for gaining a working knowledge of the Bible in three years.

3.
Learn the references

Always learn the reference while memorizing the verse, or else you will end up in confusion, with a lot of Scriptures in your mind but no idea where they are located. Someone has compared this process to associating names with faces. You can get by without remembering names, but you will find it much better if you learn to call people by their right name. In fact, the little extra time it takes to learn the references may also sharpen your memory for names.

4.
Memorize
three verses
a week

Three verses a week is a time-proven ideal for Scripture memory. More than that tends to be confusing to recall over a period of time, and less than that often fails to keep you interested in Scripture memory. At one period of my memory program I got eager and accelerated to six verses a week. To this day, the hardest verses for me to recall accurately are the ones I learned at that time. Three verses a week give you ample time to learn them thoroughly with excellent recall.

5.
Date and
record each
verse

It is a good policy to put the date you begin learning a new verse on the back of a card. You should also keep a record in your Bible study notebook in case you ever lose your pack of verses.

6.
Read the
verse aloud
and picture it
in your mind

The easiest way to memorize a new verse after writing it down on your card with its subject and reference is to read it aloud ten times, photographing it carefully in your mind as you read it. After the tenth time close your eyes and mentally picture the entire verse. Say it aloud from memory, looking at the card only when necessary. After you have said the verse successfully several times without resorting to the card, you are ready to go on to the next verse.

The ideal policy, if you have enough time, is to learn your three verses the first day of each week. This way, when you can say all three of them without help, you are reasonably sure that by reviewing them three or four times a day you can retain them easily by the once-a-day review method to be explained. Memorizing three new verses can usually be done in 30 minutes, and the rest of your review program can ordinarily be done in your spare time, as long as you carry your "current" verses with you.

7.
Review daily

Educators tell us that "review is an aid to learning." It is imperative that you review your current week's verses several times a day, particularly at the first of the week. You may have said a new verse three times perfectly and put it in your once-a-day group. But the first time you miss a word, bring the verse forward to your "current" section to be reviewed several times a day.

8.
Review for seven weeks

The secret of lasting memorization is to review each verse daily for seven weeks. It has been discovered that if you do this, then you can remove those verses to a once-a-week program for seven months, after which you can drop them into a once-a-month review.

Someone has said, "Review a verse daily for seven weeks, once a week for seven months, then once a month for seven months and you will remember it for life." I have found that I have to review verses once a month indefinitely or they may cause some trouble in recall.

A handy way to arrange your verses for review is as follows:

Current Daily Pack

Not more than 21 verses divided into two groups (rubber bands make good dividers).

1. Three current verses and those missed during last review—review three to four times daily.
2. Eighteen verses you review once daily.

Once-a-Week Pack

After the eighteenth week of your program, you should add three new verses a week to this group for seven months.

Once-a-Month Pack

It will take about nine months to start putting verses into this group, but by the time you do, you will be convinced of the worth of this program of Scripture memory.

Topics and Verses to Learn

A.   The following verses are the minimum that every new Christian should know.

Topic	Set I	Set II	Set III
The Word—Commanded to Learn	Josh. 1:8	Matt. 4:4	Col. 3:17
Assurance of Salvation	1 John 5:11,12	John 5:24	Rom. 8:1
Obedience—The Key to Happiness	John 13:17	Luke 11:28	Psa. 119:1,2
The New Life in Christ	2 Cor. 5:17	John 10:10b	Col. 2:6
Witnessing—Commanded	Acts 1:8	1 Pet. 3:15	2 Tim. 4:2
Daily Prayer Is Essential	John 15:7	John 16:24	1 Thes. 5:17

B.   This next set of verses will help you to intelligently share your faith.

Topic	Set I	Set II	Set III
God Loves All Men	John 3:16	1 John 3:16	Rom. 5:8
All Men Are Sinful	Rom. 3:23	John 3:19	Rom. 3:12
The Results of Sin	Rom. 6:23	Heb. 9:27	Rom. 5:12
Christ Paid for Man's Sin	1 Cor. 15:3,4	1 Pet. 3:18	Gal. 3:13
Salvation Is a Free Gift	Eph. 2:8,9	Rom. 3:24	Titus 3:5
Christ Is the Only Way of Salvation	John 14:6	John 10:9	Isa. 53:6
Man Must Receive Christ Personally	John 1:12	Rev. 3:20	John 5:24
Man Must Make Christ Lord of His Life	Rom. 10:13	Rom. 10:9,10	Acts 16:31

Topics and Verses to Learn

C.   This section shows the results of becoming a Christian.

Topic	Set I	Set II	Set III
Pardon from Sin	1 John 1:9	Eph. 1:7	1 John 2:1,2
Peace with God	John 14:27	John 16:33	Isa. 26:3
A New Nature	1 Pet. 1:23	Eph. 4:24	2 Pet. 1:4
New Power Within	Col. 1:11	Eph. 3:20	Zech. 4:6
Victory over Sin	1 Cor. 10:13	1 John 5:4,5	2 Cor. 2:4
Victory over Worry	Phil. 4:6,7	2 Tim. 1:7	1 Pet. 5:7
Victory over Anger	Eph. 4:30-32	Psa. 37:8	Ecc. 7:9
Victory over Depression	1 Thes. 5:18	Col. 1:12	Psa. 100:4
The Holy Spirit	Rom. 8:14	John 14:26	1 Cor. 2:12

D.   This group shows the new challenge that faces you as a Christian.

Topic	Set I	Set II	Set III
To Separate from the World	1 John 2:15,16	2 Cor. 6:17,18	Rom. 12:2
To Follow Christ	Luke 9:23	1 John 2:6	1 Pet. 2:21
To Go and Witness	Matt. 28:19,20	Acts 1:8	1 Pet. 3:15
To Grow in Faith	Heb. 11:6	Rom. 4:20,21	Acts 27:25
To Walk in the Spirit	Gal. 5:16	Eph. 5:18	Col. 3:16,17
To Be Generous	Luke 6:38	2 Cor. 9:7	1 Cor. 16:2
To Yield Yourself to God	Rom. 12:1,2	Rom. 6:13	Rom. 6:16
To War a Good Warfare	Eph. 6:10,11	2 Tim. 2:3,4	Eph. 6:13
To Seek Christian Companions	1 Cor. 15:33	Prov. 4:14	Psa. 1:1

Topics and Verses to Learn

E. These verses show what new characteristics you can expect to find in your life.

Topic	Set I	Set II	Set III
Love	John 15:12	John 13:35	1 Thes. 3:12
Joy	Jer. 15:16	John 15:11	1 Pet. 1:18
Faith	Eph. 6:16	Jas. 1:6	Rom. 5:1
Humility	Rom. 12:3	1 Pet. 5:5	Jas. 4:10
Patience	Heb. 10:26	Rom. 12:12	Jas. 1:4
Wisdom	Matt. 7:24	2 Thes. 3:15	Jas. 3:17
Grace	1 Cor. 1:4	1 Pet. 4:10	1 Cor. 15:10
Comfort	2 Cor. 1:3,4	John 14:18	John 14:1
Forgiveness	Matt. 6:14	Mark 11:25	Luke 17:4

F. These verses include essential teachings you should know about certain subjects.

Topic	Set I	Set II	Set III
God	Psa. 14:1	Prov. 1:7	Rom. 1:20
Jesus Christ	Phil. 2:9,10	Col. 1:15,16	Heb. 1:1-3
Christ's Resurrection	1 Thes. 4:14	1 Pet. 1:3	Eph. 1:20
The Word of God	2 Tim. 3:16,17	Heb. 4:12	2 Pet. 1:21
The Second Coming	John 14:2,3	1 Thes. 4:16,17	Titus 2:12,13
God Rewards Faithful Service	2 Cor. 5:10	1 Cor. 3:13	Rom. 4:10
The Will of God	Matt. 12:50	John 7:17	Eph. 6:6
Good Works	Eph. 2:10	Heb. 10:24	Titus 2:7
Heaven	Matt. 6:20	Luke 10:20	2 Cor. 5:1
Man's Ways Are Not God's Ways	1 Cor. 2:14	1 Cor. 1:18	Rom. 11:33

Additional Verses to Memorize

The above listing of verses was not intended to be exhaustive. It is only intended to introduce you to the wonderful world of Scripture memory with the hope that you will continue it all through life. These are, in my opinion, the most important subject categories and most important verses in those categories that all young Christians should know. Since the first edition was published, a number of readers have written to ask my suggestions on additional verses to learn.

Personally, I think that by the time a person learns these 150 verses, he is mature enough to find his or her own. That can be done in one of two ways. The first way is to make a list in your journal or daily diary notebook of verses that especially speak to you while reading through the Scriptures. You should always put a subject title next to the verse so it is easily added to the category of verses you have learned. Another way is to look up some more verses in your concordance or in the Thompson Chain-Reference Bible.

One thing you may consider: My assigned lists are low on prophetic passages or verses on future events, which make up almost 30 percent of the Bible. I saved most of those for the companion of this book, *Understanding the Last Days,* formerly titled *How to Study Bible Prophecy for Yourself.* If you do the 36 prophecy studies I recommend in that book, you will find the most important passages on prophecy in the entire Scriptures. This would be wise, since our generation may well be the one that is destined to see the fulfillment of those end-time events. Select from 30 to 50 of these verses and their subjects to add to your list of verses to memorize.

13

It's a Matter of Time

Well, that about winds it up. Now you realize you can study the Bible for yourself and, if you do, you will become a strong and effective Christian. What will it cost you? *Time*— or will it?

How Much Time?

Earlier in the book I stated that there are four basic ways to study the Bible for yourself. The following formula will show the minimum time required to do each properly.

Daily Reading + Bible Study + Learning = 35 Minutes

Daily Reading	Bible Study	Learning	35 Minutes
15 minutes daily	15 minutes daily or 30 minutes 3 times weekly	30 minutes weekly and then spare moments daily	Daily or 4 hours and 5 minutes weekly

At first glance, 35 minutes a day (or 1/41st of a day) may seem like a lot of time from a busy schedule. But what would you think if I said it wouldn't take any time at all? That's right, it won't cost you one single minute—in the long run. Remember this: *God is no man's debtor.* That is, whatever we give God, whether time, talent, or money, He multiplies it and gives it back to us. Many Bible verses teach this. For example, consider:

> Seek ye first the kingdom of God and his righteousness, and all these things shall be added unto you (Matthew 6:33).

> Give, and it shall be given unto you; good measure, pressed down, and shaken together and running over shall men give into your bosom. For with the same measure that ye measure shall it be measured to you again (Luke 6:38).

A peculiar thing happens when we "honor God with the firstfruits" of our time through daily Bible study: He so blesses and makes productive the remaining moments of our day that we don't miss the time; in fact, we actually gain time. It amounts to this: 23½ hours blessed by God because we spent 35 minutes in His Word will be more productive than 24 hours spent without His blessing. Similarly, four hours a week spent in reading, studying, and memorizing God's Word will so anoint the remaining 164 hours in your week that you will be more productive than you are in the 168-hour weeks when you neglect the Word of God. The God who multiplied the lad's lunch and fed 5000 men is equally able to multiply our time when we give Him the first portion.

Once you learn God's system of economics and realize that He is a multiplier of time, it won't be hard for you to be consistent in your Bible study, for then you will have found the secret of time conservation.

A busy sales executive, when asked how he could afford to spend 35 minutes a day in Bible study, replied, "I can't afford not to!" And neither can you!

It is said that John Adams, who served as the first vice-president of the United States under George Washington for eight years, then served seven years as the second president of this country, was an avid Bible-reader. In writing to his son John Q. Adams (who became the nation's fifth president) when he was approved ambassador to Russia, he advised him to do as he did—read five chapters of the Bible each day: "It only takes about thirty minutes." All Bible reading and study is time well spent!

14

How to Disciple Yourself Through Bible Study

My friend Bill Kennedy was sentenced to 20 years in prison for a crime he never committed. The whole thing is such a confusing malfeasance of justice that it is hard to believe. I am convinced a liberal prosecutor went after Bill with all the power of the government because he was the publisher of one of the most conservative magazines in the country. Liberals didn't like the way he exposed some of their prominent spokesmen and set out to destroy him. Had it not been for the Lord, they would have succeeded. By the time you read this, hopefully his unfair trial will have been overturned and he will be a free man. Whether free or not, he is already a much stronger Christian with a vibrant testimony, even in prison.

The first night Bill called, I prayed for wisdom in dealing with him. He was understandably very depressed. As gently as I could, I challenged him to begin a Bible study program while in prison that would help him mature in his Christian life. Like many long-term Christians, he was a good father and husband, but very immature spiritually, and he knew it. Obviously, discipling him would be different from most of the men I have discipled through the years. For one thing, I could not call him; he had to call me. I travel a great deal, and he only had limited funds for long-distance calls. The only answer was for me to suggest some tools for Bible study and for Bill to disciple himself.

The first thing I got him into was consecutive reading of key chapters of Scripture. Because he was so depressed, I had Bill read the four-chapter book of Philippians every day for the first month and reminded him that Paul was in prison when he wrote that little book of praise. Quickly he found, "I have learned in whatsoever state (or prison) I am, therewith to be content"—a great blessing! Only another person who wrote from behind unjust prison bars could have conveyed such a blessing. Then I had him read every day for a month the five key chapters: Ephesians 4 and 5, Galatians 6, Colossians 3, and John 15. Next I added John 13–17, then the book of First John. During the first month I introduced him to Scripture memory and keeping a daily journal or spiritual diary. Then I introduced other forms of Bible study and prayer, most already included in this book.

His calls became a delight to me, for his spiritual growth was by leaps and bounds. His depression passed quickly, even though his only daughter got married while he was in prison. The best he could do in attendance was to send a ten-minute father-daughter love message by tape recording, which was played at her wedding, amid many tears. He gradually became an ardent Bible student. Since he had so much time on his hands, he would study at least one hour a day, and many days three or more hours. Bible study became his primary interest.

During his walks on the track in the prison yard he would review his memory verses and pray. God became very real to Bill; he actually told me right after Christmas in 1996 that he was glad he had been sent to prison because for the first time he had really come to know God in a personal way. It may sound unbelievable, but he actually said, "This has been the greatest Christmas I have ever had. Jesus Christ is not just my Savior, He is my Friend." He had learned the lesson of the psalmist who said, "The joy of the Lord is my strength." How did he get that joy? From his hours of study of the Word.

It wasn't long before Bill began to share Christ with other prisoners, mostly on the track as he walked. Many found Christ, and others were backslidden Christians who needed to repent of their deeds and to get back into the Word. Not only did Bill become an effective witness but he also became a discipler of other prisoners. And that is what the Christian life is really all about—learning to be a discipler of others (Matthew 28:19,20).

Hopefully you will never have to go to prison to learn that invaluable lesson, but you may be in a position where you will have to learn to disciple yourself the way Bill did. Naturally it is better if there is someone around who will mentor you or disciple you, but that is not always possible. It is my conviction that you can disciple yourself by applying the principles of Bible study already outlined in this book. The following steps will prove helpful.

1.
Read three to ten chapters daily and keep a daily spiritual diary

We have already seen that reading is the foundation of all learning. That is so true in the lessons God would have us learn. Buy yourself an inexpensive 5 × 9 spiral-bound notebook and start keeping a daily journal (or spiritual diary) of God's special messages to you each day. Or you can reproduce the daily spiritual diary forms in the back of this book, punch holes in them, and keep them in your notebook.

2.
Start memor-
izing at least
three verses of
Scripture with
the subject title
and reference
every week

The key to memory is to review all your verses daily for seven weeks, then put the first verses in a "review weekly" file for seven weeks. After that drop them to "monthly only," bringing them back weekly only if you forget part of them. Within one year you will have many verses hidden in your heart for life.

3.
Do a Bible
study as time
permits, at
least three
times a week

Choose from any of the types listed: chapter analysis, subject analysis, Psalms study, character analysis, etc. You can use some of the charts in the back of this book or use a section of your spiral journal.

4.
Develop
a daily
prayer life

We have not said much about prayer so far because this is a book about Bible study. But if you are going to grow and mature in your faith, you will have to establish a time to pray, preferably on a daily basis. Personally I think it is even more important to read, memorize, and study the Bible than to pray, for it is more important for God to talk to us than for us to talk to Him. We certainly are not going to tell Him anything He does not know, but He has much in His Word that He wants us to learn.

However, prayer is essential for the growing Christian, for through it we learn to fellowship with God as well as share our heart's burdens openly with Him. Surprisingly, just because we know how to talk does not mean we automatically know how to pray. Most Christians have to be taught how to pray. The easiest method I know is the one taught by the Navigators, the best disciplers of Bible-taught Christians in the country today. They use the simple acrostic ACTS.

Adoration: Begin your prayer with worship or adoration of God. David did this in his psalms. As you read the book of Psalms, pick out a few you can use as springboards to adoration and use them in your prayer.

Confession: Before proceeding further, examine your heart since you last prayed, and confess all known sin. If you don't, it is futile to pray further, for as the psalmist said, "If I regard iniquity [sin] in my heart, the Lord will not hear me" (Psalm 66:18). Fortunately, we can confess our sin and know that He will forgive us of "all unrighteousness" (1 John 1:9).

Thanksgiving: It is incredible how many times in the Bible God links prayer and thanksgiving. As a counselor for many years I cannot exaggerate how important it is to learn to be thankful. It is a part of the spirit-filled Christian life (Ephesians 5:18-21) and is essential to becoming a happy person, whether in prison or as a free man or woman. Very honestly, thanksgiving is what turned my friend Bill's cell into a place of rejoicing. First, thank God for who and what He is, and then for what He has done for you and what you are learning from His Word.

Supplication: This is just a fancy word for asking God for the needs of your life and for those of the people He lays on your heart. Most spiritual leaders recommend the making of a prayer list so you don't forget anything. By the end of the first month you will have such a long list that you cannot pray for all the people on a meaningful basis every day. So I suggest that you compose A, B, and C lists. A is for your most urgent concerns. B is for the regular things you want to remember, and C is for the requests that do not need to be remembered every day. Always leave room on the right-hand side of your list to write "fulfilled," including a brief description of how that prayer was answered.

Then include a "DO TODAY LIST." This way God can guide you in the planning of your day. You can put this list on a card and clip it to today's space in your calendar. You will be amazed at how much more you will get done when you give God those valuable moments in the morning and when you consult Him while planning your day.

Spiritual Maturity Is Not Automatic

Often I have been asked what makes the difference between Christians: Some seem to grow rapidly while others hardly grow at all. The answer is really quite simple: Some are very disciplined about Bible reading and prayer and try to be obedient to His will as they find it in His Word. I don't care who you are—you will not grow unless you feed on God's Word regularly.

God gives us all the same thing when we are "born again": We all become "new creatures" or baby Christians. John called that early status of the Christian life "little children." Then he labeled the next group "young men." They had obviously experienced growth in their Christian life, because he said, "You are strong, and the Word of God abides in you, and you have overcome the wicked one" (see 1 John 2:12-14 NKJV). Obviously these "young men" of the faith had learned to overcome the temptations of the devil through their study of the Word. The third category of Christians were the "fathers," which implies maturity and reproduction. John said, "You have known Him who is from the beginning."

Note the progression: "Little children whose sins are forgiven." All you can say for these spiritual babies is that they are saved and their sins are forgiven. The "young men," however, are overcomers. They have overcome evil. This doesn't mean they are perfect—just mature enough to overcome more than be overcome. The "fathers" are really mature; they win souls and know God in a personal or experiential way. In each case the secret to growth is the study of the Word of God.

In this day when most Christians have more Bibles than they can use, there is no excuse for spiritual immaturity. Yet we all know Christians who are still "little children" after many years because they have never studied the Bible for themselves—and it shows in their immature lives. We also know other young Christians who are already "young men" of the faith because they have developed a hunger for studying the Bible, and in so doing they have "become strong, and the Word of God abides" in them.

It reminds me of Clancy Ross, my PT instructor at Las Vegas Army Air Base (now Nellus Field). He was a young man, five feet eight inches tall, who took the well-coordinated body his parents gave him at birth and through good nutrition and weight-lifting built himself up to the point that he was selected as Mr. America for that year. The Christian life is like that. God gives us our "new nature"; we are all born into God's family as "little spiritual children." Then it is up to us to build up that new faith with the Word of God until we become mature.

As you can see from this chapter, it isn't hard; God has given us the tools, and all it takes from us is time and self-discipline. You are today as spiritually strong as you want to be. It's entirely up to you. Or, as the apostle John said, "You are strong through the Word that abides in you."

How to Disciple Others

Discipleship is what Christianity is all about. Jesus commanded His disciples (and us through them) to "go therefore and make disciples of all the nations . . . teaching them to observe all things that I have commanded you" (Matthew 28:19,20 NKJV). That is not only the responsibility of ministers and missionaries, but it is also the task of all Christians. Christianity is not just about winning other people to Christ but also about helping these young Christians become disciples who take the challenge of making others disciples as well. That is the secret of the amazing growth of Christianity through the centuries—making disciples who can pass this message on to others.

You are either someone's disciple or are a discipler of others, or else you are not a very effective Christian. Hopefully, by following the techniques of the last chapter you can disciple yourself so you can learn firsthand how to disciple others. We have seen that few people have the self-discipline to disciple themselves. Most people need someone more mature than themselves to help them as a spiritual mother or father until they become "strong in the Word." That can be done singly, the way Paul discipled Timothy, or in a small group, the way our Lord discipled the twelve.

Very honestly, I have done it both ways. Having been taught by the Navigators the one-on-one method, I found myself discipling seven men individually. It wasn't long before I learned that my growing church and family made more demands on me than I could supply and still effectively make seven one-hour visits with individual men each week. So I pulled them together and found that this approach was equally beneficial. That group grew until I met with two different groups of as many as 50 men on a weekly basis. A few men dropped out, but some of the most effective and lasting work I did as a spiritual leader was to disciple men who were willing to keep their assignments and meet with me once a week.

Looking back over the more than 35 years I spent in pastoral ministry, I can tell you that the most influential and life-changing work I saw accomplished in those years was not accomplished through my preaching, or founding and administering educational organizations, or conducting over 800 Family Life Seminars, but it was in discipling hundreds of men in small groups. Many of these men are in Christian work today as ministers, missionaries, or educators, and all of them are more effectual men, fathers, and Christians than they would have been otherwise. The interesting thing is that you don't have to be a minister to disciple others. Ask God to bring you a man or woman whose heart He has touched, one who wants to become strong in the Lord.

Start with One-on-One

Until you have successfully discipled several individuals one-on-one, you are probably not qualified to start with a small group. For that matter, you don't need to from the standpoint of time. So master the technique of "one-on-one" and then follow the same procedure when your schedule demands that you work with a group. The following suggestions, using the Bible study techniques already given in this book, will prove helpful.

1.
Select a
regular time

Usually you should choose the same time each week. I found that early in the morning before men go to work or on Saturday was the best. Some people can get away for a quick lunch during the week. One hour should be enough if you avoid letting it become a chat session.

2.
Begin with
prayer

You might ask if your disciple had some answers to prayer in the past week, particularly any you had on your list. This punctuates your prayer with thanksgiving as well as requests.

3.
Ask him for a
report from
his spiritual
diary

If he has been consistent in doing his assignment on at least five days he will have enough entries to share with you of how God spoke to him from His Word.

4.
Ask him to
quote his
memory
verses

Sometimes give the reference and sometimes the subject; in each case he should supply the rest. Be sure in the early stages to demand perfection. By correcting all omitted or added words, you teach him to be accurate. During the first three weeks you should have him quote each verse. After that select six or seven verses, which lets you know he is learning them all.

5. Examine his chapter analysis or subject analysis or other Bible study assignment

This way you know he is really following through on his assignments to study the Word. Don't be surprised if he needs encouragement in the early days. Before offering a criticism or suggestion for improvement, be sure to commend him for something. Soon the Bible becomes addictive to those who study it regularly, and they feel incomplete if they don't do it on most days.

6. Ask him if he had any witnessing opportunities during the week

At first he may not have any, but as the Word begins to work in his life, they just "happen." Get him used to sharing such an experience with you and then share one or two of your own. Eventually he will need some training in soul-winning so he will know how best to handle opportunities to witness when they arise. "The Four Spiritual Laws," designed by Bill Bright, is excellent. The "Romans Road," used by many Bible-believing churches, is also a great tool, as is Evangelism Explosion by Dr. D. James Kennedy. It is best to share the presentation you have personally found the most helpful.

7. Go over his prayer life since you last met

On the first visit teach him how to pray as shown in the previous chapter, and then watch how he works his A, B, and C lists. Gradually you will see what is most important in his life. Don't hesitate to talk candidly about his prayer life; ask him to share some of his heaviest prayer requests. Be sure to write down in your notebook the request and date he shared it, so that when it is answered you can remove it by writing in "ANSWERED" and the date.

**8.
Give him an assignment for next week**

Human memory and human nature being what they are, don't leave anything to chance; carefully write out his next assignment. He should also write it out when you do. Of course, you will keep your copy in your own notebook for your next session.

The assignment will consist of:

> A. Bible reading (and the keeping of the daily spiritual diary)
> B. Three Scripture verses to memorize
> C. The Bible study you choose
> D. Prayer requests and eventually a list of unsaved souls he is praying for.

**9.
Conclude with a time of prayer together, where both of you pray**

Since spiritual infants will have to learn to pray aloud in front of someone else eventually, why not begin with you? Gradually you will see his spiritual growth reflected in the prayer, then in his Bible study, and eventually in his soul-winning.

Small-Group Discipling

Your first small group will probably grow out of your one-on-one meetings as the men or women in your group begin to lead others to Christ and want them to join in. For example, suppose three people in your group lead one or two others to the Savior and want them discipled. Assign a meeting time for them to bring their friends to the group and follow the same procedure as above, except that you will need at least 30 more minutes to allow for discussion of what they have written into their spiritual diaries and the Bible study you assigned.

One of the first assignments I always used was a study of First John. Have them read it every day for 30 days and make a list of the 27 things you can know as found in those five chapters. They make for wonderful discussion. Allow the same amount of time for Scripture memory as the one-on-one sessions, except that you can skip around. The students have to be prepared, for they won't know what verse they will be asked to quote. The peer pressure is very helpful. You will, of course, need more time for prayer with a larger group, but they will find it very effective to "bear one another's burdens" through prayer. In a small group you should make prayer voluntary, but watch the group carefully so that eventually even the most timid ones pray, even if you have to ask them to lead at times.

I learned an important rule for the nondiligent who loved the fellowship of the group but did not do their assignments. We established the policy that you could not enter into the discussion unless you had kept your spiritual diary on at least five of the seven days between sessions. One thing to remember about guidelines like that: If you make them, enforce them. If you think they are too burdensome, don't ignore them, but remove them. You will find that a simple rule or guideline will help raise the consistency of the undisciplined. Everyone needs accountability, and it won't be long until your little group becomes accountable to each other.

Gradually your group will grow from three to 12 or 18. At that point you might reorganize and try to get the most recent additions to join the new group so you can lead the mature group to more advanced work.

It's Worth It All

What I have described above will take a lot of your time and creativity. Start with two hours or more for preparation and conducting each group meeting, multiply that by four or five groups, and you are investing a big chunk of your life in these "disciples." But when you see some of them begin to set up their own discipleship groups or meetings, you will realize that you have discovered a powerful way to reproduce your life.

Someday, when you stand before the Savior at the judgment seat of Christ (see 2 Corinthians 5:10 and 1 Corinthians 3:9-17) and watch your spiritual great-grandchildren receive their rewards, you will be eternally pleased that you not only learned how to study the Bible for yourself but that you also learned how to teach others to teach others to study it for themselves! And then just imagine how you will feel when the Savior turns to you and says, "Well done, good and faithful servant; enter into the joy of your Lord!" I know what you will say to yourself: "It was worth it all!"

Additional Study Charts

. . . For your use. Feel free to photocopy them
for yourself and others

Bible Character Study

Character _____ **Main Scripture Passage** _____
Date _____

"These things happened unto them as examples unto us."

1. List other passages regarding his life. _____

_____

_____

2. Briefly describe his childhood, parents, family, education. _____

_____

_____

_____

_____

3. What character traits do you see in him, both good and bad? _____

_____

_____

_____

_____

4. Describe his main encounter with God. _____

_____

_____

_____

_____

5. Who were his chief companions? Were they a help or a hindrance? _____

_____

_____

_____

_____

6. How did he influence others? _____

_____

_____

_____

_____

Bible Character Study

Character _____ Main Scripture Passage _____

Date _____

7. What significant mistakes did he make? _____
_____
_____
_____
_____

8. Did he acknowledge and confess his sins? _____
_____
_____
_____
_____

9. What were his chief contributions in service to God? _____
_____
_____
_____
_____

10. Describe his family life. Was he a good parent? _____
_____
_____
_____
_____

11. How did his children turn out? _____
_____
_____
_____
_____

12. What is the primary lesson of his life that is profitable to you? _____
_____
_____
_____
_____

Book Study

Name of Book _____ **How Many Times Read?** ____

Date _____

1. Author: _____

2. What were the circumstances of the author when writing? _____
_____

3. To whom was the book written?_____

4. Tell something about them: _____
_____
_____

5. Where written? _____

6. When written?_____

7. Why written?_____
_____

8. What were the major problems?_____
_____
_____
_____

9. What solutions were given? _____
_____
_____
_____

10. What was the central meaning in that day? _____
_____
_____
_____

11. What is the central meaning today? _____
_____
_____
_____

12. Additional comments:_____
_____
_____

Book Study

Book _____ **Date** _____

Summarize the main theme: _____

_____

_____

_____

Pick a key verse: _____

_____

_____

_____

Outline: _____

_____

_____

_____

_____

_____

_____

_____

_____

_____

_____

_____

_____

_____

_____

_____

_____

Chapter Analysis

1. What is the main subject?_____
_____
_____
_____

2. Who are the main people? _____
_____
_____

3. What does it say about Christ? _____
_____
_____
_____

4. What is the key or main verse?_____
_____
_____

5. What is the central lesson? _____
_____
_____

6. What are the main promises? _____
_____
_____

7. What are the main commands?_____
_____
_____

8. What error should I avoid? _____
_____
_____

9. What example is here? _____
_____
_____

10. What do I need most in this chapter to apply to my life today? _____
_____
_____

Chapter Outline

Chapter _____ **Date** _____

Summarize the main subject: _____

_____

_____

_____

_____

_____

_____

_____

_____

_____

Select the key verse: _____

_____

Outline: _____

_____

_____

_____

_____

_____

_____

_____

_____

_____

_____

_____

_____

_____

_____

Daily Spiritual Diary

Week of _____ to_____

"I have esteemed the words of his mouth more than my necessary food" (Job 23:12).

Sunday: Passage _____ Date _____

God's message to me today:_____

A Promise from God   A Command to Keep   A Timeless Principle

_____   _____   _____

_____   _____   _____

_____   _____   _____

How does this apply to my life? _____

Monday: Passage_____ Date _____

God's message to me today:_____

A Promise from God   A Command to Keep   A Timeless Principle

_____   _____   _____

_____   _____   _____

_____   _____   _____

How does this apply to my life? _____

Tuesday: Passage_____ Date _____

God's message to me today:_____

A Promise from God   A Command to Keep   A Timeless Principle

_____   _____   _____

_____   _____   _____

_____   _____   _____

How does this apply to my life? _____

Additional Comments _____

_____

_____

Daily Spiritual Diary

Wednesday: Passage _____ Date _____

    God's message to me today:_____

_____

     A Promise from God   A Command to Keep   A Timeless Principle

    _____   _____   _____

    _____   _____   _____

    How does this apply to my life? _____

_____

Thursday: Passage _____ Date _____

    God's message to me today:_____

_____

     A Promise from God   A Command to Keep   A Timeless Principle

    _____   _____   _____

    _____   _____   _____

    How does this apply to my life? _____

_____

Friday: Passage _____ Date _____

    God's message to me today:_____

_____

     A Promise from God   A Command to Keep   A Timeless Principle

    _____   _____   _____

    _____   _____   _____

    How does this apply to my life? _____

_____

Saturday: Passage _____ Date _____

    God's message to me today:_____

_____

     A Promise from God   A Command to Keep   A Timeless Principle

    _____   _____   _____

    _____   _____   _____

    How does this apply to my life? _____

_____

Additional Comments _____

Jesus' Life and Teachings

Passage_____ **Date** _____

1. Is the passage about His life or His teaching? _____

2. Give the essential details of the events. _____
_____
_____
_____

3. Who were His friends? _____
_____

4. Who were His enemies? _____
_____

5. Why were they opposed to Him? _____
_____

6. What other passages tell the same story? _____
_____
_____

7. What other details do they include? _____
_____
_____

8. What do you learn about His deity in this passage? _____
_____
_____

9. Everything Jesus did expressed the nature and attitude of God. What did you learn about God in this passage? _____
_____
_____

10. What principles did He teach? _____
_____
_____
_____

11. What can you apply to your life? _____
_____
_____

Jesus' Parables

Name of Parable_____

Passage_____ Date _____

   1. What circumstances led up to this teaching, if any?_____

   _____

   _____

   _____

   2. Prepare a brief summary of the parable. _____

   _____

   _____

   _____

   3. List any additional details given in parallel passages. _____

   _____

   _____

   _____

   _____

   4. Does He give an interpretation? _____

   _____

   _____

   _____

   5. What is the one central truth He is teaching?_____

   _____

   _____

   _____

   _____

   6. Is there something here for me to apply to my life? If so, how can I do it? ___

   _____

   _____

   _____

   _____

   _____

   _____

   _____

Proverbs Study

(The Proverbs were written to make man wise toward God and man.)

1. What is presented as wisdom? _____

_____

_____

2. What negatives are condemned? _____

_____

_____

3. What positives are commended? _____

_____

_____

4. List the timeless principles. _____

_____

_____

_____

5. Do you know any other passages that say the same basic thought? _____

_____

_____

_____

6. Is there anything you have been doing that is here condemned? _____

_____

_____

7. Is something taught here that you need to incorporate into your daily life? __

_____

_____

_____

Proverbs Study

Proverb _____ **Date** _____

(The Proverbs were written to make man wise toward God and man.)

1. What is presented as wisdom? _____
_____
_____
_____

2. What negatives are condemned?_____
_____
_____
_____

3. What positives are commended? _____
_____
_____
_____

4. List the timeless principles._____
_____
_____
_____
_____

5. Do you know any other passages that say the same basic thought?_____
_____
_____
_____
_____

6. Is there anything you have been doing that is here condemned?_____
_____
_____
_____

7. Is something taught here that you need to incorporate into your daily life? __
_____
_____
_____

Psalms Study

Passage_____ Date _____

1. To whom is this Psalm addressed? _____

_____

2. List the blessings and the conditions for receiving them._____

_____

_____

_____

3. What promises did you find? _____

_____

_____

_____

4. Are there any commands?_____

_____

_____

5. Is there anything that causes you to think particularly of Christ in this Psalm?

_____

_____

_____

6. What is the gist of the Psalm?_____

_____

_____

_____

_____

7. What central thought appeals to you? _____

_____

_____

_____

_____

8. What does this Psalm teach that you can do to be a happier or more blessed
   person? _____

_____

_____

_____

_____

Psalms Study

1. To whom is this Psalm addressed? _____

_____

2. List the blessings and the conditions for receiving them. _____

_____

_____

_____

3. What promises did you find? _____

_____

_____

_____

4. Are there any commands? _____

_____

_____

5. Is there anything that causes you to think particularly of Christ in this Psalm?

_____

_____

_____

6. What is the gist of the Psalm? _____

_____

_____

_____

_____

7. What central thought appeals to you? _____

_____

_____

_____

_____

8. What does this Psalm teach that you can do to be a happier or more blessed person? _____

_____

_____

_____

_____